Don't Forget
The Child

Sermons For Advent
And Christmas

Alex A. Gondola, Jr.

CSS Publishing Company, Inc., Lima, Ohio

DON'T FORGET THE CHILD

Copyright © 2001 by
CSS Publishing Company, Inc.
Lima, Ohio

Scripture quotations marked (NRSV) are from the *New Revised Standard Version of the Bible*, copyright 1989 by the Division of Christian Education of the National Council of the Churches of Christ in the USA. Used by permission.

Scripture quotations marked (RSV) are from the *Revised Standard Version of the Bible*, copyrighted 1946, 1952 ©, 1971, 1973, by the Division of Christian Education of the National Council of the Churches of Christ in the USA. Used by permission.

Scripture quotations marked (TEV) are from the *Good News Bible, in Today's English Version*. Copyright © American Bible Society 1966, 1971, 1976. Used by permission.

Library of Congress Cataloging-in-Publication Data

Gondola, Alex A.
    Don't forget the child : sermons for Advent and Christmas / Alex A. Gondola, Jr.
        p.   cm.
    ISBN 0-7880-1834-5 (alk. paper)
    1. Advent sermons. 2. Christmas sermons. 3. Epiphany season—sermons. 4. Bible—Sermons. 5. Sermons, American—21st century. I. Title: Do not forget the child. II. Title.
BV4254.5 .G66   2001
252'.61—dc21   2001025079
                                                                                    CIP

For more information about CSS Publishing Company resources, visit our website at www.csspub.com.

ISBN 0-7880-1834-5   PRINTED IN U.S.A.

Dedicated to
my parents
Alex and Elizabeth,
who taught me the true meaning of Christmas.

Acknowledgments

Sometimes we experience Christmas at its worst: over-commercialized, expensive, exhausting, nearly devoid of spiritual significance: a Xmas with Christ "X-ed" out. I would like to acknowledge one place I have experienced Christmas at its best.

For nearly twenty years townspeople have gathered in the Cape Cod village of Dennis on the Saturday before Christmas. At exactly 5 p.m., our church bell tolls. Two-tenths of a mile away, at the Cape Cod Playhouse, a candlelight procession of up to 150 men, women, and children begins. They walk along Old King's Highway toward the Village Green. The church bell continues ringing. As they walk they sing Christmas carols. Their glowing candles flow like a river of light in the winter dark.

The procession ends at the Village Green in front of our white New England church. Candles shine through its clear glass windows. The walkers surround a replica of a stable. Around the stable a hundred luminarias (candles set in sand-weighted paper bags) are already lit.

Life-size adult and child shepherds and sheep — and a donkey named Julio — sculpted from wood by artist Walter Horak are at the edges of the stable. A magnificent angel, also sculpted from wood, is above. Joan Smith commissioned this angel in loving memory of her daughter, Cynthia. Cynthia was a Syracuse University student who was killed in the terrorist bombing of Pan Am Flight 103 over Lockerbie, Scotland. The angel's outstretched arms seem to embrace the crowd — and the world.

The Town Crier, dressed in top hat and cape, reads the story of Jesus' birth from the Gospel of Luke. On cue the Holy Family arrives. "Baby Jesus" is the newest born baby in the village. "Mary" and "Joseph" are the baby's parents. "Mary" rides in on a sway-backed pony (the veteran of fifteen Living Crèches) led by "Joseph." Children dressed as angels and shepherds also arrive on cue. The shepherds lead pigmy goats. (The goats are more "kid-friendly" than sheep.)

After the Christmas story is read and acted out the crowd responds with more Christmas carols, sung loudly in the cold night air to trumpets and trombones. Then the villagers are invited into our Fellowship Hall: sometimes for a children's play or display, always for refreshments prepared and served by our Youth Fellowship.

A procession through village streets, lights shining in the darkness, scripture read, heard, and lived out, families and new life celebrated, an angel proclaiming life and hope in the face of evil, brass sounding, carol singing, bells ringing, fellowship, community, "The Friendly Beasts," wide-eyed children, and the birth of Jesus celebrated. The Dennis Village Living Crèche is Christmas at its best to me. It's a yearly reminder of the simple beauties of Christmas. I'm grateful for the townspeople who keep this tradition alive. Their Christmas spirit helped inspire this book.

Others have helped me experience Christmas at its best. They include loved ones with whom Christmas is shared: my parents Alex and Betty, sisters Karen and Susan, wife Bonnie and son Andrew, and our wider family.

The members and friends of Dennis Union Church have gifted me with their encouragement and support, not only at Christmas, but also all through the year. I have been blessed with outstanding co-workers and colleagues: The Rev. Dr. Constance Bickford, Hope Hardy, Virginia Haskell, Steve Lovejoy, Nancy McKiernan, Noel Tipton, and Barbara Wells. Working with them is a gift. It has been a blessing to work again with CSS Publishing Company and editors Teresa Rhoads and Thomas W. Lentz.

Numerous writers, preachers, and professors have shaped my understanding of Advent and Christmas. I have tried to acknowledge each one. Some may have been inadvertently overlooked. If so, I beg their pardon. I'm grateful for their gifts, too.

Many traditions, people, places, and publications have helped *me* experience Christmas at its best: a *Christ*mas that puts *Christ* first. I hope this collection of Advent and Christmas sermons may bring something of that same blessing to you.

Let's rejoice in simplicity and wonder at the greatest gift ever given: the gift of a Savior, God's Son.

Table Of Contents

Christmas Sermons

Communion After Christmas

Christmas In July

Preface

"Now, when Jesus was born in Bethlehem of Judea in the days of Herod the King, behold, wise men from the east came to Jerusalem, saying, 'Where is he who has been born king of the Jews? For we have seen his star in the east and have come to worship him' " (Matthew 2:1-2 RSV). One of the most memorable elements of the Christmas story is the Star of Bethlehem. What *was* that star? Some contend it was a supernova exploding. The astronomer Johannes Kepler believed it was the reflected light of Jupiter, Saturn, and Mars lined up together — a phenomenon he once observed. Some say the star was really a comet. To others the star is purely symbolic.

No one knows for sure what happened — or didn't happen — in the heavens around the birth of Jesus. But the Star of Bethlehem makes a powerful statement to me. Shepherds left their flocks. "Kings" came bearing gifts. Angels burst forth in song. "The friendly beasts" joined in (at least according to the old carol). And even the outer reaches of the solar system did their part in proclaiming and celebrating the birth of God's Son.

So should we. For Christmas, the Incarnation, Emmanuel, God with us, is a light shining in the darkness. No amount of darkness can ever overcome it. The Light of the World keeps shining. And wise men — and women — still seek it.

Like the Wise Men, you and I are invited to draw ever nearer to the Child of Bethlehem: not only at Christmas but all year. May you find something of the Light of Christ reflected in these sermons. I hope your journey brings you closer to Christ. And that, like the Wise Men, star-struck with wonder, we too will find ourselves bowing down to worship him "in exceeding great joy" (Matthew 2:10b RSV).

9

Adventuring Into Advent

Isaiah 40:1-5

About twenty miles northwest of Edinburgh, Scotland, on the Firth of Forth, is the village of Linlithgow ("Linlithgo"), where the Stuarts maintained a palace. Mary, Queen of Scots, was born there. Sometime around 1500, one of the Stuart Kings, James the IV, established a tradition. He, the king, plus his royal entourage, would leave London in time to arrive at Linlithgow by December 6. Then the king and his court would enjoy themselves hunting, fishing, and partying every single day from December 6 to Christmas Eve. After a brief break for worship on Christmas morning and again on Christmas afternoon, they would return to the business of feasting, which continued without a break until Epiphany on January 6. It was a solid month of celebration. Only then would the king return to London and the business of state.

Commenting on this custom, George Bass writes, "[This has] been the popular nature of Advent ever since ... Christians in America have been able, through opportunity and prosperity, to keep Advent as kings and queens once did, instead of keeping watch for the King of kings" (*The Gift, the Glitter and the Glory*).

Isn't that largely true? For many of us, this month between Thanksgiving and Christmas is primarily a time for parties, purchases, and presents. And of course some businesses would like us to begin our shopping even sooner. This year I was surprised to see artificial Christmas trees and Christmas decorations on display in some stores beginning November 1. It makes me wonder.

Earlier generations of Christians did not observe Advent in this manner! For 1,500 years, the weeks before Christmas were considered a solemn season, a holy time marked by prayer, penitence and — get this! — daily fasting. Many of us put on pounds during this season! Earlier generations of Christians took them off

— through fasting. Our "fasting" generally doesn't start until after January 1, when, as a New Year's resolution, we may go on a diet. Weddings were discouraged during Advent. Choir processions were generally silent. Christmas decorations weren't hung until Christmas Eve. Purple was the color of the season: a somber, serious color meant to remind us of sins. Most of the Advent hymns were written in a mournful, minor key. Advent was called "The Winter Lent," and, like Lent, for a while at least, Advent was six weeks long.

Quite a difference in Advent customs from earlier generations to today! For 1,500 years, Christians prepared for Christmas, not by filling their days and nights with more and more activities, but by slowing things down, "shutting things down," so they had time for spiritual reflection, for looking inward, for anticipating the coming of Christ.

It seems to me that, to some extent, that attitude of keeping Advent apart helped make Advent an "adventure." There are, after all, several definitions of the word "adventure." The most common is "a risky undertaking." But another definition of "adventure" is "a remarkable and exciting experience." Observing Advent in the right spirit can make these four weeks before Christmas a spiritual "adventure": a remarkable and exciting time of drawing nearer to God.

For Advent is, first of all, a time of anticipation. We look forward not only to the birth of the Christ Child at Christmas, but also to that great day when the Risen Christ shall come again, when the King, the "Lion King" of Judah, will return with majesty and power. (See Revelation 5:5.) Isn't it an adventure ... isn't it exciting to believe that Christ will come again — and who knows, maybe *this* Advent! — and overturn all the suffering and pain and evil that plagues us in this world?

Gregory Fisher is a missionary who teaches at a Bible college in West Africa. He writes about an incident that took place in one of his classes when he was helping his African students understand the Second Coming of Christ. The fourth chapter of 1 Thessalonians is one place where Paul discusses the return of Christ. They were discussing that passage in class. Verses 16 and 17 read like this: "For the Lord himself will descend from heaven with a cry of command, with the archangel's call, and with the sound of the trumpet ... And the dead in Christ will rise first; then we who are alive, who are left, shall be caught up together with them in the clouds to meet the Lord in the air" (RSV). Stirring, exciting imagery written by Paul.

His students read that passage and one of them wanted to know exactly *what* Christ would say when he returned. The student took the passage literally. Since it *said* Christ will return with a shout of command, the student asked, "Professor Fisher, please tell us *what* Jesus will shout."

Gregory Fisher, their teacher, had no answer for that question. Scripture doesn't tell us. No one could possibly know. But Fisher thought about the question for a moment. He thought about all the pain and suffering he saw daily in Africa: the lack of adequate medical care, the starvation, the filth, the beggars, the orphans, the lepers, the violence, the tribal wars. And he thought about all the evil there is in the rest of the world: wars, inhumanity, genocide, economic exploitation, pollution of the environment.

Gregory Fisher responded, "When Jesus returns, he will shout 'Enough!' " Seeing that his students were startled by his answer, the professor explained. "Enough! Enough suffering. Enough starvation. Enough terror. Enough death. Enough indignity. Enough lives trapped in hopelessness. Enough sickness and disease. Enough time. *Enough!*"

The old hymn says, "When Christ shall come with shout of acclamation and take us home, what joy shall fill our hearts." Advent is a time of anticipation. We look forward to Christ's return, the Second Coming, when God will say, "Enough!" and put an end to all the suffering and injustice in our world. I think that's something of an "adventure": to be watching and waiting expectantly for the return of the Risen Christ.

But, secondly, Advent is not only a time of anticipation. It's also a time of preparation. That same Holy Christ, the Mighty King who is coming, who will say "Enough!" to the evil out there in the world, has also seen quite enough of *our* sins. Your sins. My sins. Our sins. Advent calls for us to look hard at the ways we've been

13

living, to question our values, to consider how we have been treating other people. Advent calls us to examine *ourselves*, to prepare *ourselves*. Then, when we see we've been going in the wrong direction, to repent. That's what "repentance" means. It simply means "turning around."

All of us have a choice: we can either live orientated toward sin, or live orientated toward God. Whichever part of ourselves that we feed more, with our time and energy and attention, will grow. Reminds me of the English cuckoo. That's a bird, the English cuckoo. In England it's a rather common bird. I am told that the cuckoo never builds a nest of its own. When it feels an egg coming on, the cuckoo finds another nest with eggs in it and no parent bird watching over it. Then the cuckoo flies into the nest, hurriedly lays its egg among the other bird's eggs, and flies off. That's *all* the cuckoo does in terms of parenting!

Say it's a *thrush* nest. The mother thrush returns and, not being very good at arithmetic, doesn't notice that there's an additional egg in her nest, even though the cuckoo's egg is much bigger than her own eggs. She sits on all the eggs until they hatch. Let's say four tiny thrushes and one huge cuckoo bird are hatched. The baby cuckoo will be three or four times the size of a baby thrush! But for Mother Thrush, it doesn't matter. If it's in her nest, she considers it hers.

Mother Thrush, being a good mother, flies off every morning, early, to get a worm. She flies back and sees four tiny thrush mouths opened up and peeping — and one giant cuckoo mouth. Guess who gets the worm?

The cuckoo gets bigger and bigger, and the baby thrushes get smaller and smaller. I'm told that in England, it's fairly easy to find a baby cuckoo in a nest. Simply walk along the hedge row and look for little dead baby thrushes on the ground. The cuckoo, as it grows bigger, throws them out one by one. Mother Thrush will end up feeding a cuckoo that's three times as big as herself. (Reported by Stuart Briscoe, "Preaching Today" Tape 135.)

Sin, once it gets into our lives, has a way of taking over, growing larger, and sometimes consuming us. That which we feed will grow. If we nurse, "feed" our anger, bitterness, revenge-seeking

14

pride, greed for power or possessions, self-destructive habits or behaviors, belittling another person, using another person, lust, self-pity, whatever, these things can begin to consume us and perhaps eventually *destroy* what is best within us. Advent is a time for preparation, for examining ourselves, *before* Christ returns. Self-examination, confronting old habits, changing patterns, turning back to God, *feeding* what is good and spiritually healthy in ourselves — there can be "adventure" in that.

Anticipation and preparation are two of the themes of Advent. We can "comfort" ourselves, as Isaiah puts it ("Comfort my people") with the assurance that Christ is coming again. Human beings and this planet have suffered enough. Enough is enough! Christ is coming again to set things right.

But Advent is also a time of "preparing a way for the Lord," leveling the hills, lifting up the valleys, and smoothing out the rough places in our lives, so that when Christ does return, he will find us ready to come into his presence. Anticipation and preparation: part of the adventure of Advent.

When God Comes Near

Philippians 2:5-11

Years ago King George VI of England paid a visit to one of his subject colonies in Africa. And the whole population of this African country was really, really excited. You see, a visit from royalty was unheard of. We can get a sense of the people's excitement if we could imagine being told that one of the members of the British Royal Family would be attending *our* worship service today. Wouldn't *we* be "twittering"? Well, in the country King George was visiting, the people were excited, too.

In that country there was an old shopkeeper who lived on a side street, far away from the downtown area the king was to visit. This shopkeeper had made plans weeks in advance to close his store so he could join the tens of thousands who would gather in the city square to welcome the king.

But two days before the king arrived, this shopkeeper had a minor accident, and he knew he wouldn't be able to stand on his feet very long in a crowded public square. Still, he took comfort in the fact that King George's speech would be broadcast over the radio. So on the appointed day, the shopkeeper closed up his business and made up his mind that, no matter what happened, he would not leave his radio until the king's speech was over.

About an hour before the king was to make his appearance, he traveled by motorcade toward the center of the city. There was some extra time, so the king instructed his driver to go out into the countryside so that he could see for himself how the common people lived. The king noticed this little shop and ordered his driver to stop. Then King George VI, King of Great Britain and Northern Ireland and Emperor of India, got out and rang the bell.

But the old shopkeeper was in back, glued to his radio, and even though he heard the bell, he didn't respond. You see, he didn't want to miss the king! George VI rang the bell again and called out, "Is anybody home?" The shopkeeper said to his little boy, "Go out and get rid of that guy! I'm not leaving this radio for anything or anyone!"

So the little boy went to the front and answered the door. The king asked him for a drink of water, which the boy got. They had a brief conversation and the king left.

Soon the king's speech came over the radio. He began, "I haven't learned a lot about this country yet. And I really haven't had a chance to meet many of its people. But the ones I've met have been very kind and very friendly." Then he went on to talk about his visit to a little shop on a side street, and how he met a little boy. He described the whole incident on the radio, right down to the street address.

How shocked the shopkeeper must have been when he heard that! To think the king had come to *him*, to his own shop, and he didn't even know it! (Story told by Robert H. Schuller in *The Infinite Possibilities of Little Beginnings*, Hour of Power booklet.)

I think the tragedy of tragedies is this: some people will live and die, and never really *know* God. God comes very near to all of us very often. God is as near to us as the ocean is to a fish that swims within it and is supported by it. God is as near to us at all times as the air we breathe, that's both around us and within us. But sadly, even though God is very near, we don't always "see" God or experience the Presence of God.

Perhaps we are waiting for some tremendous emotional experience, an angel visitation, trumpets blaring, the sky opening, or something else dramatic to alert us that God is near. We don't recognize that God often chooses to come to us in quiet, simple, unassuming, even seemingly insignificant ways.

So it was with the Incarnation, the coming of God in the person of Jesus. None of the contemporary historians bothered to write Jesus' birth date down. No news crews rushed to the stable to capture live footage of the birth of this Baby. Even in Bethlehem itself, virtually all of the population was unaware that anything of earth-shaking significance had happened on that night.

The busy world of Jesus' day just went about its business. No one has recorded exactly what Caesar Augustus was doing in the

18

Imperial Palace in Rome on that particular evening. But whatever Caesar was doing, you can bet he and his advisors felt it was of supreme importance. If the angels had come to Caesar instead of the shepherds and said, "Leave all this alone. It doesn't matter. Nothing matters except the fact that a poor Jewish teenage mother is giving birth to a baby boy in a stable," you would have bet that Augustus would have thought he was the victim of some practical joke.

God came near in the Incarnation. But most of the people of Jesus' day didn't know it, because God chose to come to us in such a quiet, simple, and unassuming way.

This reminds me of another true "royalty" story. When Queen Victoria lived in Balmoral Castle in Scotland, she sometimes liked to walk through the surrounding countryside incognito: no heralds, no guards, no retainers, no ladies in waiting, just John Brown, her faithful servant, following at a discreet distance behind her. One day, while on one of these "walkabouts," Queen Victoria came across a flock of sheep being driven by a boy. The queen accidentally got in front of the flock of sheep. When that happened, the boy shouted, "Get out of the way, you stupid old lady!"

Queen Victoria smiled, said nothing, and moved on. Her servant came along, scandalized, and told the boy he had just insulted Queen Victoria. "Well," said the boy, "if she expects to be treated like a queen, she ought to dress like a queen!"

God comes near to us at Advent and Christmas, quietly, unassumingly, gently, *not* "dressed up" in the robes of royalty but in the form of a tiny baby. How "unKinglike!" How "unGodlike!" God comes subtly, compared to all the tinsel and trappings of this time of year: no Madison Avenue press agent, no advertising flier, no clever television commercials. Just the story of the birth of a baby in Bethlehem.

But don't be misled by the Baby's humility, God's "self-emptying," his servant nature. His name is the Name which is above every name. And a Day is coming when every knee shall bow before him, in heaven and on earth and even under the earth, and every tongue *will* confess that Jesus Christ is Lord! (Philippians 2:7-11).

him? The One who is born among us? The One
...urning? Have we experienced the presence of Jesus
God does come near, especially near, though hidden
...the wonderful trappings of this season, in the lovely
...s decorations, like these Chrismons in our sanctuary, in
o... ...ent wreaths and banners, reminding us that Jesus Christ is
the Light of the World, in the gift giving, speaking to us of God's
Gift of Jesus, in the joyous special music, in the evergreens, proclaiming God's eternal Love, in the excitement and wonder in the
shining eyes of a little child.

How can we find this "God Come Near"? We need to open
our hearts and our eyes and look around, with expectancy and
wonder. Back in October, "Ginnie" Haskell, in her wonderful La-
ity Sunday sermon, recommended two books by Roger Von Oech:
A Kick in the Seat of the Pants (Perennial Press), and *A Wack on
the Side of the Head* (Warner Books). "Kick" has a suggestion that
is pertinent. Roger Von Oech asks us to take a moment and look
around us and find five things that have the color blue. Go ahead
and do it: find five things in this sanctuary that are blue. With
"blue" in mind, you will find that blue seems to be jumping out at
you *everywhere*: someone wearing a blue tie, a woman in a blue
dress, the pretty blue in the chandelier. People tend to find what
they are looking for.

This past July, Bonnie and I had the opportunity to travel to
London. While there we spent a morning visiting St. Paul's Cathedral, certainly one of the great architectural and artistic creations
of Western culture. While at St. Paul's we spent a lot of the time,
with hundreds of other tourists, looking up — up at the soaring
ceilings, the huge columns, the magnificent dome. We spent so
much of our time looking up that we each got a "crick" in our
neck.

But, in a quiet moment, we looked around, at floor level, and
found something easily overlooked. It was a replica of Holman
Hunt's famous painting of Jesus Christ as "The Light of the World."
Most of us are familiar with this painting. It shows Jesus, looking
rather like this (show Jesus figurine). Notice again the color blue!
Jesus is standing outside the fast-closed door of the believer's heart,

quietly, gently, humbly waiting to be invited in. But there's no latch on his side of the door! We're the ones who have to open the door!

Our King is coming to *us* in Advent and Christmas. The King of kings and Lord of lords is coming to our community, our church, our homes. He's coming quietly and humbly. Are we looking for him? He's coming looking for admission to our lives. Are we ready to let Him in? If we're not careful, we might overlook him in the busy business of this season.

Are we ready to admit the God who comes near?

Peace In Our Time?

Isaiah 2:1-5

Let there be peace on earth
And let it begin with me ...
Let us walk with each other
In perfect harmony.

Let peace begin with me ...
To take each moment and live each moment
In peace eternally.
Let there be peace on earth
And let it begin with me.

Do you recognize these words to a familiar hymn? It's a lovely sentiment, isn't it? But is it realistic? Oh, I *know* that around Christmas especially, we talk about peace. We proclaim that Jesus, the "Prince of Peace," is coming. And we sing carols with beautiful, peaceful images in them: "Peace on earth and mercy mild, God and sinners reconciled"; "O little town of Bethlehem, how still we see thee lie." (Bethlehem, of course, being a region that has experienced very little peace in more than fifty years.)

Lovely sentiments. Beautiful images around Christmas. But are we being *realistic*? Is it reasonable to hope for "Peace in *our* time?" Let's face it, a world at complete peace doesn't seem very likely, does it? I once read an estimate that in the roughly 4,000 years of recorded history, something less than 300 of those years, about eight percent, have been essentially "peaceful": years where there have been no major wars or conflicts. According to this estimate, the vast majority of history, 92 percent of the time, nations in our world have been at war.

Frankly, I think that's a fairly optimistic statistic, don't you, that there has been peace as *much* as eight percent of the time? I'm surprised that there have been *any* peaceful years at all! Take the

23

present time. At this moment, our country is in the happy circumstance of *not* being engaged in an armed conflict. And right now there are some genuinely hopeful developments on the international scene: positive steps toward a peace treaty in strife-torn Northern Ireland, the essential end of the Cold War, the re-targeting of United States and Russian nuclear missiles away from each other's cities and out to sea, possible portents of a peace treaty between the Israelis and Palestinians. I'm always hopeful and a little bit excited when I read about developments like these.

Still, there's plenty of bad news in the paper, isn't there? In Israel, Yitzhak Rabin, a Nobel Peace Prize winner, was gunned down minutes after attending his country's largest ever rally for peace. When he was reached, a blood-stained copy of the peace song he had just sung was in his coat. And still, at this moment, though our country is at peace, there are dozens of armed conflicts raging around the globe: mostly civil wars, but some, like the war in Africa, exceptionally ugly. Here and there are flickers of light in the darkness, little glimpses of a world at peace. But the darkness around us is still quite deep, isn't it? This year has been a better year, all told. But there still is no "peace in our time."

But *can* there be? Is world peace, not just eight percent of the time, but a majority of the time, maybe most of the time, even possible? I believe it can be. I believe that because God has promised us peace. And God does not lie.

So we *sing* "Let there be peace on earth." We long for "peace in our time." We trust in God's promises. But how can it begin to happen? First, for there to be peace in our time, or in God's time, by maintaining a vision of peace. Visions have power. Visions change things. Often, what we envision starts to come about.

In one of his many books, *A Savior for All Seasons* (Fleming H. Revell Company), Bill Barker makes that point. Dr. Barker tells the story of a bishop from the East Coast who paid a visit to a small religious college in the Midwest. The bishop stayed at the home of the college president, who also served as professor of physics and chemistry. After supper, the bishop and the young college president got into a discussion about the future of the world. The bishop contended that the Millennium *must* be coming. You

see, he believed that just about everything that could be
ered about nature had already been discovered and that just
everything that could be invented had already been invented
reasoned the bishop, Christ would certainly return *soon.*

The young college president/professor disagreed politely. He
contended that there were *many* more positive developments yet
to come. When the angry bishop challenged the president to name
just one, the president replied he was certain that within just fifty
years human beings would be able to fly.

"Nonsense!" sputtered the outraged bishop. "Only angels are
meant to fly!"

The bishop's name was Wright, and he had two boys at home
who would prove to have greater vision than their father. Their
names were Orville and Wilbur Wright (pages 175-176).

Walter Wink, a noted Bible scholar, writes: "Everyone now
seems aware of the helpfulness of visualizing. The basketball coach
asks the players to mentally 'see' the ball going through the hoop.
The holistic healers ask their patients to 'see' their cancer being
healed. We need the vision of a fairer, peaceable world. We need a
hope to believe in, to struggle for." Wink continues, "We can today choose faith or paralysis. What we choose may well deter-
mine the future of the earth" (*Christian Century*, March 3, 1982).

And so, if we want peace in our time, or in any time, we need
to hold fast to the vision. Fortunately, our scripture lesson from
Isaiah offers us one of the greatest visions of peace ever offered in
the long history of the world. It's the vision of swords and spears,
weapons of war and destruction, being transformed into plows and
pruning hooks, into the tools of production. It's the vision where
our investment in things that kill is changed into an investment in
things that bring life. Having that kind of vision for our world *can*
help begin to turn things around.

But if we are to have peace in our time, or at any time, more
than just having a great vision is called for. There is effort in-
volved in making that vision happen. Beating swords into plowshares is *work.* Peacemaking is *work.*

The *work* of peacemaking is well pointed out, I think, in that
wonderful statue inspired by these verses that stands in at the United

Nations Plaza. Have you ever seen it? A powerful man is swinging a heavy hammer high above his head, ready to smash it down on the sword he is holding with his other hand. Swords don't readily change into plowshares. They have to be beaten. And we human beings, so accustomed to war-making, and our societies, all of them so fearful of each other, so invested in weapons, will probably also have to be beaten to change. But with God's help, swords *can* be beaten into plowshares. And we can change.

Some time back, there was a wonderful article in the *Cape Cod Times* about new uses for spy satellites. The headline read "U.S. Spy Satellites Shift Gaze from Tanks to Trees" (November 28, 1995). The author went on to detail how some of these remarkably sensitive satellites, which we used for decades to spy on the Soviets, are now being redirected. Their targets are no longer military sites but areas of sensitive ecology around the globe. The satellite data is being used to study ecological threats, to monitor the weather, and to help improve agriculture. A perfect example of turning a "sword" into a "plowshare" for the benefit of peace. It can be done.

And in the end, it will be average citizens, like you and me, pursuing the vision of a world at peace, that will encourage the world's governments to make the shift from war-making to peace-making. An old "War Horse," President Eisenhower, expressed it like this shortly before his death: "I'd like to believe that the people in the long run are going to do more to promote peace than our governments. Indeed, I think that people want peace so much that one of these days governments better get out of their way and let them have (peace)."

What can you and I *do* to help promote peace? We can pray for it, we can read how to promote it, we can vote our conscience as it pertains to peace, we can write our representatives, we can write letters to the editor, we can support causes that work toward peace. We can hold fast to the vision of a peaceful world.

Will there be peace in our time? I don't know. But there will be peace in God's time. God has promised it and God will not fail us. Will we work with God to do what we can to "beat swords into plowshares and spears into pruning hooks"?

Let there be peace on earth. But let it begin with me!

The Peaceable Kingdom

Isaiah 11:1-9

Edward Hicks was a rough-and-tumble carriage maker who lived in Pennsylvania in the early 1800s. His younger years were spent in wild living, hard drinking, and bar room brawls. But at age 23, Hicks had a dramatic conversion. Troubled, he stumbled into a Quaker meeting. And the peace and quiet intrigued him. He gave up drinking and brawling and became a Quaker. Soon afterward Edward Hicks received a call to preach.

Quaker preachers are not paid. For years Hicks traveled from town to town, preaching at small meetings. He supported himself by painting signs. Eventually, he quit preaching and took up painting full time. In the end, unschooled, untrained, unsettled Edward Hicks became the leading folk artist in America in the early 1800s.

His most popular painting was *The Peaceable Kingdom*. Hicks painted it as many as 100 times. This one image seemed to capture and compel him. Each rendition was slightly different, of course. But a child, an ox, and a lamb appear in each one. They live at peace with wild beasts: lions, and tigers, and bears.

Someone once said, "When the lion lies down with the lamb, *only* the lion gets to sleep well!" Someone else said, "That picture is great, as long as you replace the lamb every day!" Actually, the most dangerous figure in the picture is not the wolf *or* the lion, but the baby. Wolves and lions have a lot more to fear from us than we have to fear from them. But in Edward Hicks' Peaceable Kingdom, there was neither predator nor prey.

Hicks' painting is more than engaging art. It's a political/religious statement. William Penn of Pennsylvania always appears in every painting. Penn is often off in the distance, negotiating a peace treaty with Native Americans.

William Penn was Edward Hicks' hero. Hicks believed the path of pacifism and religious tolerance — the way of William

Penn — would create Philadelphia, a city of brotherly love on earth. If *only* we would live like William Penn, thought Edward Hicks, then certainly the Peaceable Kingdom could be established *here.*

But perfect peace wasn't established by William Penn. Penn was a good Governor. But he only governed Pennsylvania for two years before he sailed back to England, returning only once. His deputies governed Pennsylvania poorly in Penn's absence. Philadelphia, "The City of Brotherly Love," became stressed with dissention and strife. William Penn could not usher the Peaceable Kingdom in.

Twenty-five hundred years before Edward Hicks picked up a brush, people in Jerusalem *also* dreamed of a Peaceable Kingdom. Their hopes rested on the slim shoulders of King Hezekiah. Hezekiah was only 25 years old when he ascended to the throne.

At his coronation, Isaiah, the court prophet, offered the moving vision we heard this morning. Isaiah saw this idealistic, young King — who may have been his student — as filled with the Spirit of God. Hezekiah would know and do what was right. The poor would be treated fairly. The wicked would be punished. Peace would break out between nations — and in all of nature, too. If only Hezekiah would listen to God's Word, reasoned Isaiah, then surely the Peaceable Kingdom would come.

Hezekiah was a good king. He was a religious reformer. He tore down the high places where idols were worshiped. He was often in repentance, fasting, and prayer (see 2 Kings 18-20).

Still, Hezekiah took risks that enraged his powerful enemies and endangered his nation. Judah was invaded several times during his reign. The Peaceable Kingdom did not come in by Hezekiah.

Recently a new theme park, The Animal Kingdom, was opened at Disney World in Orlando. The Animal Kingdom hosts over 1,000 different animals from 300 species. There are 2.3 million carefully cultivated plants.

At the center of The Animal Kingdom is The Tree of Life. The Tree of Life is fourteen stories tall. Its trunk is fifty feet wide. It has 8,000 fake branches with 100,000 fake leaves sewed to them. Its canopy stretches 160 feet across the sky.

Disney describes The Tree of Life like this: "A powerful symbol representing the interconnected nature of all living things ... Carved into the gnarled roots, enormous trunk and uplifted branches are the twisting, turning shapes of more than 300 animal(s) ... "

Disney continues, "Every guest is invited to stroll The Tree of Life Garden through the root system of The Tree of Life. This soft landscape is filled with otters, flamingos ... lemurs, tortoises, and colorful ducks, storks, cranes and cockatoos." Or, the guest may enter a theater built into the roots of The Tree of Life. It's currently showing the movie, "It's Tough to Be a Bug."

Near The Tree of Life, "safaris," jeeps pulling little open cars, venture into the "wilds" of Orlando. Cheetahs, Nile crocodiles, elephants, hippopotami, and black and white rhinoceri can be viewed — in safety, of course. The Tree of Life, with its surrounding garden, and human beings and animals in harmony: it sounds a bit like the Garden of Eden, complete with computer-controlled artificial mist that rises up on cue!

But, for all its clever engineering and special effects, Disney's Animal Kingdom is *not* the Peaceable Kingdom either. Before the park opened, thirty of the imported animals died. They couldn't adjust to the climate. Even now some of the animals hide most of the day from the sun — and from the tourists. The jeeps sometimes run over the smaller creatures. One wonders if air pollution affects the animals. Even the magic of Disney and all the wonders of technology can't create a Peaceable Kingdom on earth.

Yet that image of a Peaceable Kingdom persists deep within us. Maybe that's why Edward Hicks painted that one image, again and again. Maybe that's why we respond so well to Hicks' painting. Maybe that's why we look with hope and expectation to new religious and political leaders. Maybe that's why millions will pay billions to see an artificial Eden in Orlando.

Our vision of a Peaceable Kingdom is a yearning for Paradise Lost. That image of a Garden of Eden, where all things work well, is deep in our souls. We know it's not here yet. The poor (some of them) get welfare but do not fare well. Human society is still filled with injustice and strife. Wolves still eat lambs. And we human beings continue to make a mess of nature.

29

Still, we long for the Peaceable Kingdom. When will it come? The Kingdom will come in its fullness when Christ comes again. *Jesus* is the "shoot" that grows out of the stump of Jesse. *Jesus* is the One the Spirit of God rests upon. *Jesus* lived his whole life in "the fear of the Lord," in obedience. *Jesus* lifted up the poor and put down the oppressors. *Jesus* is the Little Child whose gentle ways will lead us. *Jesus* is the Lion of Judah (Revelation 5:5) and the Lamb of God (John 1:36). Even the sharp contrasts of nature come together in him.

The Kingdom of God is coming with Christ. But the Kingdom of God is already *here*! Every time Edward Hicks painted his painting, every time William Penn preached peace, every time King Hezekiah judged fairly, a bit of the Kingdom was established. Every time we use technology wisely, every time we reach out to the poor, every time we stand up for justice, a bit of the Kingdom comes. Every time we are guided by the Spirit of God, every time someone fights to save a wolf or a lion, every time we join in communion, a bit of the Kingdom is among us.

The Peaceable Kingdom is God's dream for creation. God, in God's goodness, has allowed us to share that dream. Longing for it and looking for it and working for it is good. That's part of what we do at Advent. We look back. We look around us. We look forward. We pray, "Thy Kingdom come, thy will be done, on earth as it is in heaven."

One day — may it be soon — there *will* be a Leader who judges fairly, stands up to oppression, and redeems the poor. One day — may it be soon — the wolf *will* lie down with the lamb. One day — may it be soon — a little Child *will* lead all of creation.

Christ has come. Christ is here now. Christ will come again: our Advent song!

Be Prepared!

Romans 13:11-14; Matthew 24:36-44

Have you noticed that, over the last decade or so, there have been *lots* of predictions about the end of life on this planet — at least the end of life as we know it? We were warned a few years back that using spray deodorants could destroy the ozone layer. We have been threatened with global warming and a melting of the polar ice cap that could change the world's climate — with disastrous results. We have been warned about the dangers of over-population, with its resulting competition, famine, social disintegration, and disease. Back in May of 1994, when a giant comet struck Jupiter, astrophysicists reminded us that the same could happen to *our* planet; or that Earth could be destroyed by a meteor shower, exploded by contact with a pocket of anti-matter or swallowed up into a Black Hole. And of course, in spite of recent progress in arms control, there is *still* the threat of nuclear war. The United States and Russia still retain between them thousands of large, strategic weapons: plenty of firepower to blow the world up. Environmental disaster, nuclear war, collision with a giant comet — there have been many predictions about how the world might end.

And, as we're all aware, not only *scientists* make these predictions. Some *religious* leaders also make them. Hal Lindsay has sold over thirty million copies of his book, *The Late Great Planet Earth*, which details how Lindsay thinks the world will end. Billy Graham also has written on this subject, in his bestseller, *Approaching Hoofbeats: The Four Horsemen of the Apocalypse*.

Apocalypticism generally has not occupied a big place in many church traditions. We may not know quite what to make of these discussions. Terms some religious leaders use in discussing the End Times — Premillennialism, Millennialism, Amillennialism, Dispensationalism — may seem strange to us.

Still, the End Times are alluded to in the scriptures a lot! Perhaps as many as 400 times! And it's a theme that comes up especially during Advent every year. So, let's think again about what the Bible says about eschatology, which is the Greek word for the end of time.

The Gospel lesson for this morning, Matthew 25:1-13, that amazing little parable about the wise and foolish maidens, is one of the many places in the New Testament where there is a reference to the imminent return of Jesus. In this parable, the bridegroom represents Jesus. The maidens, both wise and foolish, represent believers, the members and friends of Christ's church. One of the points of the parable is that when Christ comes again, he will arrive unexpectedly. No one can "pin down" the day or hour of his return.

Yet, since the very beginning of the Christian church, some have tried to predict the *exact date* of the Apocalypse. The end was solemnly predicted, on the basis of Bible study, for the year 1000. And again for 1524 A.D., when a German astronomer and preacher named Stoeffler predicted that a flood was coming that would wipe out everything. Stoeffler convinced his parishioners to build arks and rafts. When the water didn't rise as predicted, they threw Stoeffler into a pond. The End was predicted again in 1843, when a New York farmer named William Miller convinced his followers to sell everything they owned and to don white robes and wait for Christ on hilltops. It was predicted again in 1900 and again in 1910, when Haley's Comet came near. In 1977 a group of 24 believers in Arkansas held a ten-month vigil in a small house, waiting for the Apocalypse. They finally were evicted when the mortgage wasn't paid.

There were many specific predictions as we approached the year 2000, particularly around the potential for a Y2K crisis. But so far every specific prediction has proven wrong. It's enough to believe that Christ *will* return. But of the specifics of God's calendar, Jesus says, "You know neither the day nor the hour" (Matthew 25:13 NRSV).

In the parable of the wise and foolish maidens, Matthew compares the Day of Christ's return to the joy, excitement, and celebration of a wedding feast. The Rule of Christ will be preferable to the things we know, just as day is preferred to night or the warmth of springtime is preferred to the cold of winter. It's good to know that humankind's long, twisted, and often bloody history will eventually come to a positive end. Wouldn't it be much worse to believe that this world's suffering and evil will continue forever, without relief?

Hinduism believes something like that. One Hindu myth holds that every thousand years, a bird flies over the Himalayas with a silk scarf in its beak. As it passes over the highest mountain in the Himalayas, every thousand years, the scarf brushes the rocks below. When that mountain is worn to the ground by the scarf, one day of Brahma (god) is completed. And these days of god make up a cycle. And the cycle never ends.

The Christian understanding of time is quite different. We (and also the Jews and the Moslems) believe that history is not aimless or unguided. History belongs to God. History is His Story: it's going somewhere. Believing that there is a meaning and purpose and direction to history gives human life hope.

Back in 1985, a 34-year-old long-distance swimmer named Florence Chadwick waded into the icy waters off Santa Catalina Island off the coast of California. She was determined to swim from the island to the coast, a distance of over twenty miles. Florence Chadwick was no novice. She had already swum the English Channel, both ways. She was prepared for the freezing water, the long distance, and the sharks, which had to be driven off with gunfire.

What she wasn't prepared for was the fog — fog so thick she couldn't see an arm's length ahead. Florence Chadwick swam for almost sixteen hours, but then asked to be taken out of the water. Ironically, though she didn't know it, she was almost there, just a half mile from shore. The fog had blinded her eyes and stolen her courage. Seeing no end in sight, she gave up. Just two months later, on a clear day, Florence Chadwick not only completed the swim, but shattered the men's world record by two hours.

Having a vision of the future keeps us going. Sure, the future of this planet, and our individual futures, may sometimes seem cloudy, maybe even dark and forboding. But the Return of Christ is our hope. Scripture says there is a Day ahead, a Day of Rejoicing, a Day of Celebration, like a great wedding, when the Bridegroom will return. As Christians, we look forward, not to the worst, but to the best.

A final point is made by our Gospel lesson: if Christ is returning unexpectedly, we must be ready, like five of the ten young women were ready. That point was brought home to me once while standing in the pulpit of a previous church. It had been my custom to go into the sanctuary every Saturday night to run through my sermon. It was a huge ark of a sanctuary, with lots of dark wood and stained glass windows, and seventy-foot ceilings in a large complex of buildings. Kind of an imposing place to be all alone in on a Saturday night. One Saturday night, I went into that sanctuary, into the pulpit, to practice preaching. Not too long before, the Trustees had had electricians come in and install some huge arc lights near the sanctuary ceiling to light up the rose window from the inside so that passersby could enjoy it at night from the outside.

I didn't know that before those huge lights come on, they are preceded by about five seconds of an electric hum that courses through the sanctuary. Then when they come on, they explode with a flash. Well, there I was, all alone, in that dimly lit sanctuary, and the electric hum started. And my skin began to crawl, and the little hairs on the back of my neck stood up, and I looked around, wondering what was happening. Then suddenly there was this big explosion of light, illuminating the beautiful, multi-colored rose window.

For an instant I thought Christ was coming again! And I felt like one of the five "foolish" maidens because I realized I wasn't ready! Part of the message of Advent is that old Scout motto: "Be prepared!"

What does the Bridegroom want by way of our preparation? The parable tells us. Christ, the Bridegroom, wants our light to shine! The light of our faith, prepared in worship and prayer and Bible study. The light of our good deeds, feeding the hungry, sheltering the homeless, which comes out of our faith.

If the Bridegroom were to come right now, would you be ready? Would your light be shining? Would he know you enough to admit you at the door?

What we're looking forward to is something good: the joy of Christ's return, the celebration of a wedding party. No one knows when it might happen. Are you ready? Is your light shining?

Be prepared!

Who Can Endure
The Day Of His Coming?

Malachi 3:1-4

Have you ever noticed that many people seem to feel they either have "too much" Christmas or "not enough" Christmas? Television commentator Andy Rooney is one who thinks he has had "too much" Christmas. Andy Rooney, in fact, has proposed a "Christmas Holidays Limitations Act." These are some of the provisions of that Act:

1. Capital punishment would be mandatory for anyone caught selling Christmas ornaments before Thanksgiving.

2. Magazines would be prohibited from offering three Christmas editions, the first in October. No magazine dated "December" or calling itself "Christmas Edition" could be available before December 1.

3. Insurance companies, funeral homes [and] hardware stores would be forbidden from mailing out anything to anyone that said "Merry Christmas" on it.

4. [And] there would be stiff penalties for anyone caught mailing out Christmas cards before December 10 (from *And More by Andy Rooney*, Altheneum Press). Clearly, Andy Rooney feels he has had "too much" Christmas.

But then there are those who may feel they don't have enough. Counted among them might be people who, because of financial difficulties, can't buy what they would like for Christmas to give what they would like for Christmas.

Others can be lonely during the holidays. They may suffer from what has come to be known as "Seasonal Depression" or the "Holiday Blues." Dr. Lester Grinspoon, a psychiatrist at Harvard Medical School, writes, "Any clinician in mental health sees a disproportionate number of people who suffer from loneliness. [But] Christmas and New Year's *amplify* loneliness, perhaps more

37

than any other two days of the year. The holidays can be especially hard on the recently widowed or recently divorced, on shut-ins or those in nursing homes, on military personnel and others separated from their loved ones. Rather than feeling they have 'too much' Christmas, these folks may feel they don't have enough."

Well, whether your Christmas seems like "too little" or "too much," you may experience these pre-Christmas weeks as a test of your endurance. *Enduring* until the Lord comes: that's what our scripture lesson from Malachi is about. "Who can endure the day of his coming?" asks the prophet in the Revised Standard Version translation.

Only at this point, we Christians say Malachi is talking not about an impending holiday, but about the Second Coming of Christ. That's one of the great themes of Advent, the Second Coming of Christ. We believe that, because Christ came once, he's going to come again! The first time he came in humility, Mary's Baby, dependent, born in a stable, surrounded by animals, cradled in a manger. But the second time he will come in triumph, as the King of Glory, as Ruler and Judge of this world.

Something of the grandeur we should be looking forward to at Christ's return became evident to me one Advent evening last year when I watched a special titled "What Child Is This?" on public television. It was filmed at St. Olaf's College in Northfield, Minnesota. The program featured the college's symphony orchestra and 400 male and female students assembled in five choirs.

At the beginning of the program, the 400 choir members marched into the packed 4,000 seat auditorium in a grand procession, following behind a line of colorful, twenty-foot-tall Advent banners. Accompanied by the symphony orchestra, they sang the Advent hymn:

> *Lift up your heads, ye mighty gates,*
> *Behold, the King of Glory waits,*
> *The King of kings is drawing near,*
> *The Savior of the world is here.*

And the 4,000 members of the audience sang along.

So here you had 400 trained voices in five choirs, a symphony orchestra, and an audience of 4,000 all joining together in a hymn of praise to the Risen Christ. I don't mind telling you that it was a thrilling moment for me, both as a viewer and as a believer. I got mist in my eyes and a lump in my throat. When Christ comes again, he will return as the King of Glory. The grandeur of his Person will be evident to all.

But that same Day of our Lord's return is also described by Malachi as being a day of fire, a day of testing, a day of judgment. God's King is coming to clean things up. Christ can't be expected to live and rule in a squalid, sin-filled world, any more than we might expect the Queen of England, should (for whatever reason) she decide to visit Dennis, Massachusetts, to be put up in a run-down rental off of Route 28. Royalty expects and demands the best.

Malachi tells us what to expect from Christ's return by using images like these: "The Lord you are looking for will come suddenly to his Temple. He will be like strong soap, like a fire that refines metal. He will come to judge like one who purifies and refines silver. As a metalworker refines silver and gold, so the Lord's messenger will purify the priests."

The image is that there is a day of purification and rigorous testing ahead for *all* of us. Christ might return at any moment. Religious leaders will be tested. Every one of us will be tested, as gold is refined by fire.

Those of us who have been fortunate enough to have been raised in a Christian home, to have enjoyed the benefits of attending Sunday school and youth group and confirmation classes, and Bible studies and retreats, who have spent a lifetime of Sunday mornings attending worship at church might self-confidently feel we've "got it made." We'll have no problem with the Day of Judgment. Our lifetime of church involvement, our good works, our occasional acts of self-sacrifice will certainly save us.

Actually, as I understand it at least, God's judgment works on something of a "sliding scale." Those of us who have *received* a lot spiritually aren't *excused more* easily. Rather, we have *more* expected of us. "From everyone to whom much has been given, much will be required" (Luke 12:48b NRSV). That saying makes me kind of nervous. I have been fortunate enough to receive a *lot*. I've received a *lot* in this life, health-wise, family-wise, educationally, emotional support-wise, materially, in terms of opportunities to grow and develop in my Christian faith. From everyone who has been given much, much more will be demanded. I get nervous when I hear that. What about *you*? When the King of Glory comes again, he will come in grandeur, but also in judgment. Who can endure the Day when he comes?

What *is it* that God wants from us? There is a story from the Middle Ages about a young woman who was expelled from heaven. She was told she could return when she could bring back to God the one thing that God valued most. So she searched the world for what God might want most.

She collected coins given by a destitute widow for the poor. She brought back dust from the shoes of missionaries who had spread the gospel to distant lands. She even brought back drops of blood from a dying martyr. Yet every gift she brought to God was turned back.

One day she watched a small boy playing in a fountain. A man rode up on horseback to take a drink. When he saw the boy playing in the fountain, the man remembered his own childhood innocence. Then he looked into the water and saw the reflection of his hardened face. He was overcome by the sin of his life. At that moment he wept tears of repentance. The young woman caught one of those tears and brought it back to heaven. She was received by the angels with joy.

The person who will *endure* is the one who has made himself or herself *ready*. Preparing for Christ's return calls for soul-searching and repentance, two of the great, but in our society at least, often-forgotten themes of this time of year. Nothing is more pleasing to God than the gift of our sincere *repentance* — a seeing of our sins, a sadness over our sins, a willingness to try, with God's help, to amend our living, a turning back to God, a turning things around.

Those of us who feel we've had "too much" Christmas or "not enough" Christmas maybe have missed the point of Advent. Perhaps those who feel we have too much Christmas need to be reminded that this pre-Christmas period was never designed as a time of relentless, frantic activity that fills our days so full that we tend to block out God. Maybe we need to examine what we've gotten ourselves into and ask ourselves, "Is this or that activity, this or that custom, this or that social obligation helping to prepare my soul for the coming of Jesus? Is it making me more reflective, more ready?" Any honest person would have to admit that, very often, the answer will be "No."

Perhaps those who feel they have too little Christmas need to be reminded that Advent *isn't* a time for excessive gloom. Nor is it a time for *worshiping* "the ghost of Christmas past." Perhaps you are feeling lonely or discouraged or downcast about the future, maybe profoundly saddened by how things have gone for you in your life. But there is Good News on the horizon! Christ *is* coming again, maybe soon! In him every valley (including the valley of your loneliness and discouragement) *can be* lifted up. In him every mountain and hill (including the mountains and hills of your problems) *can be* made low. In him the uneven ground, the "rough places" (of your sins and my sins) *can be* made smooth. All flesh (including you, my friend) will see him together.

The Second Coming, though it be a time of judgment, is *not* a time of despair, for the same Jesus is both Judge and Savior. The One who will judge us is the One who died for us on a cross, taking all judgment on himself. *His* judgment of us is for our salvation and flows from his love. The fire of his judgment is unlike any other fire in the world. With most fires, the closer we come, the worse we are burned. With Christ, the further we separate ourselves from him and the fire of his judgment, the more it will burn. But, the closer we come in repentance, the more we are warmed and comforted by his love.

Who can endure the Day of his coming? Christmas *may seem* like an endurance test for us. And yet that is perhaps because we have missed the point of Advent. This is a season neither for excessive busyness *nor* excessive gloom, but for making ourselves ready for the Second Coming of Christ.

Lift up your heads. The King of Glory *is* coming, in grandeur and in judgment. Are you ready? If we can concentrate on making ourselves ready, then our Christmas may end up being neither too little nor too much.

Mary's Song

Micah 5:1-5a; Luke 1:39-55

It's almost here, isn't it: Christmas! Can you believe Christmas is just *four days away!* Are you ready? Of course, all of us are ready, aren't we? After all, we've been getting ready for weeks! The Christmas lights are on the house, the light-up plastic Frosty the Snowman is on the lawn. A fresh wreath is hanging from the door. The tree's up, the presents wrapped, Christmas cards mailed. Everything's ready, isn't it? Or, if it isn't, it will be soon. Because Christmas is just *four days away.*

Christmas being close, you may have come to church expecting a Christmas message. You may have expected to sing your favorite carols to familiar tunes, nice and loudly, in the "key of free." But, that's not going to happen today. Because we're still in Advent, the period of preparation. We need to be careful not to rush the birth of the Child.

So, on this Fourth Sunday of Advent, we consider the assigned readings. The little story about Mary and Elizabeth seems pleasant enough, doesn't it? We can imagine the two pregnant women, cousins, meeting in Elizabeth's country home in the hills of Judea. We can picture their excited, loving embrace. There's that lovely touch: the baby leaping in Elizabeth's womb on meeting Jesus as his greeting to Jesus. Finally, at the end of the passage, Mary breaks forth in magnificent song.

It's heartwarming, isn't it? Or is it? This morning, let's take a hard look at Mary's situation and Mary's song. They may not be as idyllic as they seem.

I wonder, first, if we don't over-sentimentalize Mary. We tend to think of her, in the words of an old hymn, as "Gentle Mary, meek and mild, (who) look(s) upon her little child." Words like "blessed," "Virgin Mother," and "kind" come to mind.

Think about the ways Mary is portrayed. I once checked a Roman Catholic religious articles store for images of Mary. The store had dozens of Marys in stock. I quizzed the clerk. In every single case, Mary is young and slim (no Ultra-Slimfast diet for her!). She's peaceful and beatific. She usually comes with a halo (which, the clerk told me, was detachable). Every Mary in the store has brown hair and blue eyes. *Every* Mary. The clerk told me all their Marys are made in Northern Italy. Apparently, most people there have brown hair and blue eyes.

Now, Mary may well have been all of the above (except brown-haired and blue-eyed; Mary was Semitic). But, if Mary *was* serene and peaceful, it was *in spite of*, not *because of* her lot in life. Mary's life was a mess.

She was poor. She was young, fourteen, maybe. She was un-educated. She was pregnant out-of-wedlock. Her fiance had lurk-ing suspicions about her pregnancy. Her mother and father aren't mentioned at all. Maybe Mary's parents were embarrassed. Maybe that's why Mary went out of town, without Joseph, for three months, to visit her cousin.

Philip Yancey writes: "Nine months of awkward explanations, the lingering scent of scandal — it seems God arranged the most humiliating circumstances possible for [Jesus'] entrance, as if to avoid any charge of favoritism." He continues, "I am impressed that when the Son of God became a human being, he played by the rules, harsh rules: small towns do not treat kindly young boys who grow up with questionable paternity" (*The Jesus I Never Knew*, Zondervan Publishing House, p. 30).

Poverty, scandal, questions at home, Roman oppression abroad, the anxieties of a first-time pregnancy, morning sickness, mood swings, crazy cravings. Then, giving birth in a stable, surrounded by animals, far away from home, with no midwives or female rela-tives in attendance. Mary's life wasn't peaceful. It was a mess.

But in the midst of Mary's mess, there was a Message. A re-minder that God particularly chooses and uses the lowliest and least. A reminder of how God selected elderly, childless Abraham and made him the father of great nations. Of how God chose Moses, a verbally-challenged, "not our kind," never-quite-fit-in-at-the-palace, hot-tempered murderer turned shepherd, and made him the deliverer of God's people. Of how God picked a quarrelsome, rag-tag collection of slaves with an attitude problem to be God's Chosen Ones. Of how God selected the little town of Bethlehem to be the birthplace of the Messiah. God has been lifting up the least and last for a very long time.

Then, in the most astonishing reversal of all, the great God who made everything became almost nothing. Philip Yancey writes again:

> ... The Maker of all things shrank down, down, down, so small as to become an ovum, a single fertilized egg barely visible to the naked eye, an egg that would divide and redivide until a fetus took shape, enlarging cell by cell inside a nervous teenager ... God emerged in Palestine as a baby who could not speak or eat solid food or control his bladder, who depended on a teenager for shelter, food and love.
> — The Jesus I Never Knew, p. 36

Mary realized that God chooses and uses what is least, lowly and little: like her! When she understood this, she forgot her worries and began to sing:

> My soul [glorifies] magnifies the Lord ... For [God] has looked with favor on the lowliness of [God's] servant ... [God] has shown strength with [God's] arm ... [God] has brought down the powerful from their thrones, and lifted up the lowly; [God] has filled the hungry with good things, and sent the rich away empty ...
> — Luke 1:46-48a, 51-53 NRSV

Mary's song is Good News for the "least" among us: for the homeless man sleeping in a shelter; for families with no health insurance who wait in line at a clinic; for the five million Americans who spend over half their pretax income on housing — often substandard; for the father who works two minimum-wage jobs and the mother who works another to provide for their kids. It's Good News for the thirteen million hungry children in America; 1.4 million in Massachusetts.

"God will lift up the lowly. God will fill the hungry with good things." If you're hungry, homeless, or hurting, then Mary's song is Good News for you!

But is Mary's song Good News for *most of us* here this morning? I wonder. Mary's Song is a very scary song to me. Listen again: "[God] has shown strength with [God's] arm, [God] has scattered the proud ... [God] has brought down the powerful ... and lifted up the lowly; [God] has filled the hungry with good things and sent the rich away empty."

James Harnish tells the story of a tourist in the Holy Land who bought a ceramic nativity set in Bethlehem. As he was boarding the plane for his return flight to America, the tourist was stopped by a security guard. The guard looked through his luggage, and asked him to unpack the nativity set.

The tourist took out the figures of Mary and Joseph, the angels, the shepherds, the Wise Men and the Baby Jesus. The guard insisted on putting each figure through an x-ray machine.

"Why?" the tourist asked. "It's a ceramic nativity set, after all!" The guard answered, "Ah, these figures could contain explosives." (*An Explosion of Joy*, December 24, 1996, Tampa, Florida). How right he was!

We Americans are "sitting pretty at the top of the world's economic pyramid" (James F. Kay, *Christian Century*, December 10, 1997, p. 1157). We are seven percent of the world's population and own 49 percent of the world's wealth. We are a nation that obsesses over being overweight, while one-third of the children in Asia and half the children in Africa suffer from malnutrition. On the average, each of us here this morning has an annual income equal to that of 58 Haitians. We are the richest, most powerful, and most well-off people that ever lived.

So, for *us*, Mary's words *are* explosive. Mary raises and praises a God who will overturn everything. We who are so comfortable on top are in danger of ending up on the bottom. No wonder John the Baptist, no friend of the *status quo*, leapt for joy in his mother's womb when Jesus came near.

Mary doesn't sing the Magnificat with malice. She's still gentle. But, Mary is not "meek and mild." Under the inspiration of the Holy Spirit, this poor, uneducated, pregnant-out-of-wedlock teenager tells it like it is. She reminds us of a theme that runs throughout the Bible: God's justice. That God *is* coming. That God will balance the scales and right all the wrongs.

So, do we dare sing Mary's song *with* Mary? Frankly, it's not easy for me. I have a comfortable home, two cars, a good job, health insurance, and a pension plan. I have enough food to eat to meet my needs. And, probably more than is good for me. Mary's song is "so pointed it sticks in my throat," wrote James Kay recently in *Christian Century* magazine (December 10, 1997). I know what he means. Most of us would prefer a nice, quiet Christmas carol, something soothing, like "Silent Night, Holy Night," over Mary's Magnificat. We don't want to hear a freedom song that threatens our comfortable world.

Still, I know in my heart that God inspired the Magnificat. I know in my heart that the great reversal will come. I know in my heart that I must begin to learn it and, more importantly, to live out what Mary sings.

It's unfamiliar to me. Fortunately, we have Mary to lead us. Like Mary, who was poor, you and I can learn to recognize the poor. They're around us. But we often prefer not to see them. Like Mary, who felt her lowliness, we can learn of our lowliness: the things we have done, the good things we have left undone, that have created pain and suffering for others.

Like Mary, who stood for the poor, we can learn to stand with and for the poor. You and I *can* feed the hungry and clothe the naked and shelter the homeless. A lot of that we can do right through our church. And if we can no longer do it ourselves, we can pray for those, and support those, and fund those who serve the poor for us. And not just at Christmas, when giving is easy, but all year. With Mary as our model, we can recognize how much the poor like her have to teach us. They have so much to give, if we would only get close and let them give.

47

So, sing your freedom song, Mary. Sing it loud and sing it strong, and we'll do our best to follow. Ultimately, your song is for, not against, us. We who sit up high and comfortable *need* to be knocked down before we can be lifted up. We need to be confronted with the truth before we can begin to change. We need to see how poor we are in spirit before we can ever become rich in giving. And we, too, need to be set free: free from an obsession with possessions. We need the freedom to care and the freedom to share.

So, let's take Mary's song to heart and try to live it. Let's let the great reversal be in our hearts and in our lives, now, *before* God's Great Reversal comes. Then maybe, just maybe, we *will be* ready for Christmas. Ready to welcome the Christ Child, who came to us poor, who stands for the poor and *for* the poor in spirit, like those of us who are hoping to change.

Witnesses To Christmas:
Mary, The Mother Of Jesus

Luke 1:26-38, 46-55

One of the greatest works of religious art ever conceived shows Mary, the Mother of Jesus, holding her dead son in her arms after the crucifixion. It is Michelangelo's sculpture, *The Pieta.* Many of us have seen it, either at St. Peter's in Rome or at the Vatican exhibition at the 1964 World's Fair at the Flushing Meadows in Queens.

When on display at its permanent home in Rome, *The Pieta* is always well guarded because some years back, *The Pieta* was attacked by a madman with a hammer. Before he could be stopped, he had seriously damaged Mary's face and one of her arms. This incident was a terrible tragedy in itself. But also a testimony: a testimony to the strong emotions, both positive and negative, that Mary sometimes engenders.

On the one hand, Mary is, for tens of millions, the subject of the most tender emotions and the deepest devotions. It is estimated that two billion Hail Marys are said every day. Five million pilgrims traveled to the grotto at Lourdes in France this past year alone, because Mary is said to have appeared there to a peasant girl in 1858. The waters of Lourdes, because of the presence of Mary, are reported to have healing powers. Accounts of Mary appearances and Mary-related phenomenon are apparently on the rise worldwide. Over fifty weeping Madonnas have been reported in Italy alone in just the last two years. Here in the United States, there is a hot-line you can call daily to get updated information on Mary, Mary sightings, and Mary's messages. The number is 1-800-345-MARY.

Devotion to Mary isn't just limited to the Roman Catholics either. Mary is mentioned 34 times in the Koran. Large numbers of Muslims travel to sites around the world on pilgrimages to Mary. Hymns to Mary can even be found in some of the new Methodist songbooks. Mary has become, as historian Karen Armstrong puts it, "a major celebrity."

Of course, there is the danger in overemphasizing Mary. Roman Catholic theologian Hans Kung writes about the dangers of a "Marian cult." Pope John XXIII found it necessary to warn his flock, "The Madonna is not pleased when she is put above her Son." But then, on the other hand, sometimes some Protestants have gone out of their way to ignore Mary altogether. References to Mary are pretty rare in most Protestant churches, limited mostly to Christmas carols or the recitation of the Apostles' Creed. She is, of course, found in our crèche sets around Christmas. But little is heard about Mary the rest of the year.

So, while there is a danger in making too much of Mary, we Protestants also need to be careful not to ignore her completely. Mary, after all, occupies a unique place in scripture. She is the only person who is depicted as being with Jesus throughout his entire lifetime. She's there at his birth. She provides Jesus a home in his childhood. No doubt, as was the custom, Jesus would have received his early religious education from her. She's mentioned in several scenes in Jesus' adult ministry. Mary is there at the foot of the Cross, and listed among the members of the Early Church in Acts (1:14). She's in Jesus' life from birth to death — and beyond death, to the resurrection and ascension. And Mary was, in her own right, clearly someone special. For God chose her, of all the women on earth in all of time, to bear God's only Son.

This morning I'd like to begin a series I'm calling "Witnesses To Christmas." I'd like to speak, week by week, about all the figures we generally associate with the birth of Jesus: Mary, Joseph, the shepherds, the angels, the Wise Men, maybe even the animals. I'm not so sure about the animals. But the major figures, for sure. I'd like us to think, week by week, as we add figures to our crèche set, about who these characters were and what they stood for. This morning we begin with Mary. Who was Mary?

In the first place, when I think of Mary, I can't help but think of her as being profoundly humble. At the time of Jesus' birth, Mary (or more likely Miriam — for that would have been the Hebrew form of her name) would have been a peasant girl in her early to mid-teens: somewhere between fifteen and seventeen years old. Mary was a teenage mother!

More than likely Mary could neither read nor write. Women were not generally offered the opportunity of an education. She was married to a poor carpenter. They lived in a backwater village. In social terms, Mary represents the great mass of common humanity. She had no special status to set her apart.

Throughout the Gospel accounts, Mary is represented as being not only humble but human. There are several incidents recorded where she simply does not understand her son. When Jesus is twelve years old and gets separated from his mother and father on a trip to Jerusalem, both Mary and Joseph misunderstand Jesus' explanation that Jesus had to be about his Father's business (Luke 2:41-52). Later on Jesus appears to rebuke his mother at the wedding feast at Cana: "O woman, what have you to do with me? My hour has not yet come!" (John 2:4 RSV). There's the incident in Mark where Mary and her other sons come to collect Jesus because they are afraid he is losing his mind (3:21, 31-35).

Mary doesn't seem perfect or perfectly sinless to me! The Gospels depict her as being an ordinary human being with quite human failings. So to me, it is fitting that Mary is pictured at the foot of the Cross. Like all of us, she needed a Savior to take away her sins. When he died on the Cross of Calvary, Jesus died equally for his mother.

Yet throughout the Gospels, Mary is a positive example. One author has called her "the true child of Abraham." If Abraham was "the Father of Faith," maybe we could think of Mary as "the Mother of Faith." Mary was devout. She was reflective. She was obedient. She was persevering. Mary is a good illustration of the very best that you and I could ever hope to become.

The Bible depicts Mary as a devoted student of the Hebrew Scriptures. The "Magnificat," which is attributed to her in Luke (1:46-55), is composed mostly of Old Testament verses woven together. Mary knew her Bible. She also obeyed it. We read in Luke (2:22-40) that she and Joseph faithfully presented Jesus in the Temple the eighth day after his birth, in accordance with the Law. Knowing God's Word, taking it seriously: that's a good example for us.

Mary is also portrayed as someone who was reflective and spiritually sensitive. She took the events of that first Christmas seriously, "pondering them in her heart" (Luke 2:19 RSV). Even at a tender age, Mary was looking for life's deeper meanings. Once again, I think Mary is meant to be a good example for us.

We encounter God's mysteries every day, especially around Christmas. But often do we take time to "ponder in our heart," to explore things prayerfully, as Mary did? Sometimes we have to before we can understand.

Most importantly, Mary is the model of obedience. The angel comes to Mary and tells her that she has found favor with God — and that God has a very special and very unusual plan for her. And, for a moment, God's plan of salvation of the entire world depends on the response of this illiterate teenage peasant girl living in Nazareth. Church historian Jaroslav Pelikan writes, "If, by her own free will, [Mary] had refused God, as Eve did, then the plan had to change. The entire plan of salvation hung in the balance ... [there] ... had to be a free and independent source of action in Mary that made this happen."

Mary's response to Gabriel, "Behold, I am the handmaiden of the Lord," was costly. She would be pregnant out-of-wedlock, a very serious situation in the Hebrew society of her day. There was more than the risk of social disapproval. There was the risk that she could lose Joseph. And if Joseph had rejected her and if the Law was strictly followed, there was the risk that Mary could even be put to death. For the punishment for a woman breaking her engagement vows with another man, in certain circumstances, was death by stoning (see Deuteronomy 22:23-24).

Yet Mary goes forward on faith, not knowing where God would lead her, even though it might be costly. Mary, to me, is a shining example of faith.

Who was Mary? A woman of faith and courage. A positive example to all of us. She represents the symbol of the kind of spirit that welcomes Jesus and enters into the closest possible relationship with Jesus.

So, "Hail Mary, full of grace." She is indeed "most blessed among women." For blessed and full of grace are those of us who, like Mary, allow Jesus to be born in them.

Witnesses To Christmas:
Joseph

Matthew 1:18-25; 2:13-15, 19-23

We continue this morning with a second sermon in the "Witnesses To Christmas" series. One by one we will consider the figures associated with a crèche set. Last week I talked about Mary, the mother of Jesus, and about what Mary might symbolize for us. I suggested that Mary is something of a universal symbol: the symbol of a kind of perfect faith, the kind of spirit that immediately welcomes Jesus and enters into the closest possible lifelong relationship with him. To me, Mary is meant to be the model of obedient faith, the "Mother of Faith."

As you can see, there is another figure in the crèche this morning. Joseph has joined Mary. Joseph is a largely forgotten figure in our celebration of the Birth of Jesus. For example, he is almost never mentioned in any of the popular Christmas carols. I checked it out. Our *Pilgrim Hymnal* has 46 hymns for Advent and Christmas. Mary, the mother of Jesus, is mentioned in eleven. Nine carols make reference to the shepherds and eight to the Wise Men. But poor old Joseph is spoken of in only one, "Christians Awake, Salute the Happy Morn!" Not a tune that most of us find ourselves humming!

Now the point here is not who's number one on the hit parade of Christmas. Obviously, Jesus is the most important and everyone, including Mary and Joseph, is secondary to him. It's just that Joseph's poor representation in Christmas carols is an indication that Joseph is a bit in the background. We may not know very much about his motivations or what he may have thought.

Still, Joseph the carpenter was a witness to the first Christmas. Like every other figure at the manger, Joseph has something important to say. This morning I'd like us to hear a little bit more from Joseph. I'm going to be making use of a first person narrative sermon about Joseph I once heard on tape. The sermon was written by Dr. Haddon Robinson, who teaches preaching at Gorden-Conwell Theological Seminary in South Hamilton, Massachusetts.[1] Please imagine, as you hear these words, that Joseph is speaking for himself.

"I think I had better introduce myself. My name is Joseph Davidson. Many of you already know me. I've been hanging around Christmas for a long time. But I suspect you don't know me very well. Sometimes I feel a bit like the father of the bride at a wedding. Nobody notices him, but he has to pay for the whole affair ... I want you to know that Christmas cost me a great deal. Let me tell you a bit about myself.

"My small claim to fame is that I happen to be a descendent of David, Israel's greatest king. That really isn't much to boast about. David lived a thousand years before I was born. By the time I came along there were hundreds, even thousands, of people who had been descended from David. Yet, it was something I was proud of, the same way that some of you are proud of being Daughters of the American Revolution. You boast a bit about tracing your family lineage back to people who came over on the Mayflower. That is sort of what it is with me.

"I grew up in the town of Bethlehem. It's a little town about seven miles south of the capital city of Jerusalem. It was difficult to make a living there. When I was a young man, I went up to the hill country near the Lake of Galilee and I settled in the town of Nazareth. I'm surprised some of you know Nazareth. It was so small it was the butt of jokes. Some of my countrymen would say, 'Can anything good come out of Nazareth?' But, I didn't go to Nazareth because it was a great city. I went there to work my trade.

"I'm a carpenter ... Carpenters are practical people. We're not poets or philosophers. I like to work with things you can handle and measure, cut and saw. I enjoy working with wood ...

"... Wood is an honest thing. I understand that some of you have doors that are hollow in the middle. I don't want to insult you, but you ought to be ashamed. I like wood that's wood clear through ...

"Times in Nazareth were good to me ... In Nazareth I first met Mary. She was about fifteen-and-a-half when I met her. Wonderful girl, wonderful woman. Before long, we were betrothed. Betrothal was sort of like engagement ... It lasted a year ... During that period, families got to know each other. They worked out a dowry. They searched the records at the temple in Jerusalem, because it would have been possible in a country as compact as ours for near relatives to marry and not even know it.

"It was a period in which I came to love Mary. She was a wonderful combination of girl and woman. There were times when she laughed and her eyes danced with joy. It was ecstasy to be with her. And as a woman she was as solid as the pillars of the temple ... She pondered life. And not only that, she could give expression to her thoughts in songs. Some of her songs were absolutely magnificent.

"That period of betrothal was a period in which I dreamed. I thought of building a house for Mary and for the children we would have. It's strange, isn't it, how quickly ... dreams can turn to nightmares? I noticed Mary had become quiet and withdrawn. When I asked her what was wrong, she told me she just couldn't talk about it. I had to go up to Capernaum to do some work, and while I was away, I wondered about her silence. I wondered if I had done something to offend her or her family.

"By the time I came back to Nazareth, I was beside myself. I asked Mary not to shut me out of her life, but I was completely unprepared for her answer.

"She ... said, 'I'm pregnant.' She began to weep. Of all the things that had been in my mind that one had never occurred to me. Pregnant! I had not been with her. If not me, who? How could this have happened without my knowing or without her parents knowing? We had love. We had trust. We had plans and dreams. Why?

"I needed to ask questions, but I was afraid to hear the answers. When she did answer me, it was like a slap in the face.

"She told me an angel had appeared to her and told her, a sixteen-year-old girl living in a fifth-rate little village, that she was going to be the mother of Israel's Messiah. Then she told me something else. She told me she was still a virgin, that the Spirit of God had come upon her and planted a baby in her womb. I was furious.

"It was one thing for her to betray our love. It was another thing to treat me like a fool by telling me a story that bordered on blasphemy. I could not believe it ... I wanted to lash out. I wanted to hurt her as she was hurting me.

"Back in the old Law, it said that if a woman were taken in adultery she should be stoned, and I could understand that law. Although we did not practice it then, I wanted somehow to get back at her for what she had done to our love, to my faith, and my reputation.

"I want you to understand that I'm a righteous man. I try to live according to the scriptures. I had a reputation in the community. As soon as they knew that Mary was pregnant, they would assume I was the father, and my reputation would be destroyed. I was furious. I was going to make it public. I was going to go before the elders at the gate and sever this relationship ...

"I couldn't do that; I loved Mary. Even though my trust was shattered, and I felt I could not marry her, I would not expose her to public shame. I decided that I would sever the thing quietly and make up some kind of a story.

"Mary knew she had to leave Nazareth. She knew that the caustic gossip in that community would be impossible to stand. She decide to go ... to live with her cousin, Elizabeth.

"After Mary left, however, I couldn't get her out of my mind. I'd ... work at my bench, but I could not pay attention to what I was doing. I could not eat; I could not sleep. One night I had a dream. I dreamed I was walking through a dark place, and suddenly, there up ahead of me was a blinding light. In the center of that light, I saw an angel. I was terrified, and the angel told me not to be afraid. The angel said, 'Joseph Davidson, don't be afraid to take Mary as your wife because this child she bears is of the Holy Spirit. And you shall call his name Jesus, because he will save his people from their sins.'

"When I awoke from that dream, I was elated. I had a message from heaven. I realized that Mary had told me the truth ... I apologized to Mary for doubting her word, and as soon as we could, we were married. I swear to you in all that time, I never touched her ...

"When I was young, I thought that if once in my life I were to see an angel, just one angel ... I would never doubt. I would always believe. I saw an angel. It was in a dream ... it was real and vivid to me.

"To be honest with you, Jesus didn't seem like much of a savior of the world. Oh, he was good. He was obedient. But when he was an infant, Mary fed him from her breast. You sing that hymn, 'The poor little Jesus, no crying he makes.' He cried ... When he fell in the streets of Nazareth and skinned his knee, it bled. I held him on my lap to tell him stories, and he fell asleep. He wasn't that different.

"... I wondered. Oh, I wondered ... Some of you here have a faith like Mary's. It's obedient. It's strong. It's rich. It's devout. Some of you, I think, are more like me — practical people ... You like things you can touch, feel, measure ...

"Faith has its moods. After I was confronted by the angel, I thought I would never doubt again. But there were times when the whole thing didn't make sense to me. Some of you are like that. You believe your doubts. You doubt your beliefs. Sometimes you wonder if you believe at all. I understand.

"All I can say is ... when I faced ... questions, I came down on the side of faith. I *faithed* it through, in spite of my questions and my hurt ...

"And that's what God used. I, Joseph Davidson, put my thumb print on Jesus Christ. I taught him to be a carpenter. He was creative. He could make oxen yoke that were easy ... I taught him that.

"Of course, he was the Savior of the world. He put his thumb print upon my soul, but it wasn't easy. It's just that when I thought I knew what God wanted me to do, I did it. I had faith enough for that.

"That's my story ... You want to celebrate Christmas and worship again the birth of Jesus. And you ought to. But I just wanted you to know that I, Joseph Davidson, had something to do with that. When God sent his boy to earth, he put him into the care of this carpenter, who sometimes believed his doubts and doubted his beliefs, but faithed it through ...

57

"I'm not the main character of the story. But you might remember ... that God ... chose Joe Davidson, a carpenter who believed the best he could."

You might think about that.

This sermon was presented as a first-person narrative. After the introduction, I left the pulpit and changed my clergy robe for a simple burlap robe. From that point on, I "became" Joseph Davidson, loosely following Dr. Robinson's sermon. Obviously, this approach may not work for every preacher. But a lay speaker might also personify Joseph.

1. Quotations from "Joseph Davidson: The Neglected" by Dr. Haddon Robinson. Available from *Leadership Journal's Preaching Today* audio/print series, tape no. 126. Used by permission.)

Witnesses To Christmas:
The Shepherds

Luke 2:8-20

This is the third in our "Witnesses To Christmas" series. This morning the children added four shepherds and thirteen sheep to our crèche set. It's getting quite crowded around the manger! They join Mary and Joseph in waiting for the Baby Jesus, who "arrives" on Christmas Eve.

It's interesting to me that the shepherds are the *only* ones in the crèche scene who are there because they've been *invited*. Mary and Joseph are at manger side by virtue of their family relationship with Jesus. The Wise Men arrive at Bethlehem largely on their own initiative, by following the star. But the shepherds: the shepherds are where they are by divine invitation. God dispatched an army of angels to go and get the shepherds: to wake them up and shake them up and make sure the *shepherds* come in.

That's nice. But let's think for a moment about who these shepherds were. We may tend to romanticize them a bit. It's easy to think of the shepherds the way we generally see them in Sunday school Christmas pageants: as mop-haired, bright-eyed, little boys, dressed up in cut-out burlap bags, or maybe their dads' old bathrobes, so long they drag along the floor. They look sweet and cute, even though they might still have a slingshot in their back pocket. That's one image of shepherds we frequently have.

Or we may think of shepherds the way we see them portrayed in some Victorian paintings — as pipe-playing, sturdy, wholesome country boys: honest-looking, healthy, round, cheerful faces, ruddy complexions. And indeed, the Bible does offer us, in the Psalm 23, and in other places, that image of the noble shepherd. These solitary shepherds, who went off with their flocks for weeks, maybe even months, were generally the shepherd/owners of the sheep. They would treat their small flock, their whole livelihood, maybe a hundred sheep in all, the way loving parents care for their children. The way God cares for us.

59

But it's likely the men watching the flocks on that particular night, in that particular location, were just not that kind of shepherd. For on the hills outside of Bethlehem, just five miles south of Jerusalem, the shepherds would have had a different kind of duty. For one thing, there would have been lots and lots of sheep: thousands and thousands of sheep; at certain times of year, even tens of thousands of sheep, bleating away in a gigantic corral. Some of those sheep, the unblemished ones, would end up within the next few days as sacrifices in the Temple. The rest of them would end up in the city market as meat. Bethlehem was the last stop for these sheep.

And the men who watched them were not at all the protective and possessive shepherd owners but hirelings, day laborers mostly, something like stockyard workers today. These men were part of a social class called the *Am-har-arez*, or "people of the land." They were looked down on by polite society. On the ladder of social status, they were considered just above slaves.

James Montgomery Boyce writes about the reputation of this type of shepherd:

> *They were looked down upon ... They were despised and mistreated. They were thought to be crafty and dishonest ... So bad was their reputation that they were not even allowed to bear testimony in a court of law. It was assumed people like that would lie....*
> — *Christ In Christmas*, NAVPRESS, p. 12

They were probably not conventionally religious, either. Their duties with the sheep would keep them out in the fields on the Sabbath. So they couldn't go to worship. They would have been illiterate. So they couldn't read the scripture. Theirs was a dirty job in a dusty land. Water was scarce. So they couldn't keep up with ritual hand-washing demanded by the Law. There was a popular saying among the Jews around the time of Jesus that shepherding was a "thieves trade" that no true Jew would teach his son.

Yet *these* folks, and these folks alone — the rough equivalent of transient drifters or street people today — these folks alone receive an invitation to the first Christmas. God even sends an angel chorus out to get *them*. What does it mean?

To me, it's a witness that God has a special concern for the dispossessed, the poor, and the forgotten. Some theologians have gone so far as to argue that God has a "bias" for the poor, that God likes the poor best. And actually, when you think about it, there's a *lot* of biblical evidence to that effect.

Some years back, Ron Sider wrote a book titled *Cry Justice!* (InterVarsity Press). *Cry Justice!* is little more than quotes of Bible passages, two hundred pages in all, lifting up God's special concern for the poor.

From the very beginning of scripture, God is the One who raises up the weak and defends the downtrodden. Exodus, chapter 3, verses 7-8a (RSV):

> *Then the Lord said, "I have seen the affliction of my people who are in Egypt, and have heard their cry because of their taskmasters; I know their sufferings, and I have come to deliver them out of the hand of the Egyptians, and to bring them up out of that land to a good and broad land, a land flowing with milk and honey."*

God is the God who takes a bunch of broken slaves and chooses them and delivers them from suffering. God cares for the poor.

And centuries later, when God's people get established and become wealthy themselves, they forget the poor. So God raises up prophets to defend the poor and to warn the people of the dangers of forgetting them. Listen to the words of Isaiah, chapter 58, verse 7 (RSV):

> *... Share your bread with the hungry, and bring the homeless poor into your house; [and] when you see the naked, [give them clothing] ...*

God cares for the poor.

God cares so much for the poor that God, in Jesus, chose to *become* one. God could have become anyone God wanted to in the Incarnation. God chose to become someone who was poor.

Jesus was born in a cattle stall in an occupied country. His parents were too poor to bring the normal offering of a lamb to the Temple. They brought the offering of the poor, two pigeons, instead. For a while, says Matthew, Mary and Joseph and Jesus were refugees in Egypt. Sort of makes you think about those refugees in Rwanda, doesn't it? After that, says Matthew, Jesus and his parents came as immigrants to Nazareth. Sort of makes you think about the immigrants in America today, doesn't it?

Jewish rabbis received no fees for their teaching, so Jesus had no regular income. He told one of his potential followers, "Foxes have holes, and birds of the air have nests, but the Son of man has nowhere to lay his head" (Matthew 8:20 RSV). He had no home. When he died, the only possession he owned that had any value was the cloak he was wearing. He had to be buried in a borrowed grave, through the kindness of a friend.

You see, when Jesus says, "I was hungry, and you fed me; I was thirsty, and you gave me drink; I was a stranger, and you welcomed me; I had no clothing, and you clothed me ..." (Matthew 25:35-36a paraphrased), he wasn't speaking metaphorically. He *was* hungry and thirsty and a stranger and without enough clothing. Jesus was poor. God cares for the poor.

And so must we.

Brita Gill-Austern teaches Pastoral Psychology at Andover Newton Theological School. I remember her telling this story:

> *One Sunday I was on my way to church in the subway in Philadelphia reading and editing my sermon that I was to give that morning. I was wrapped up in my world, my worry, my self-preoccupation about how it would go. Yet I was forced to look up from my manuscript when a man walked in the subway at the next stop. He was very grubby, dirty, and had at least a three-day-old beard and generally the appearance of one you hoped would sit elsewhere. As he entered he said, "Good morning, Sally and John. Good morning." People gave him a quick glance, but no one spoke to him. At the next stop as people got on, he called out again in a most cheerful voice, "Hi, Robert and Janne, Peter and Diane."*

Still, no one looked. At the next stop he did the same thing. Once again silence. At the next stop, same thing. Again silence. Then all of a sudden he plopped himself down in front of me and said, "I recognize everybody, but no one recognizes me."

Finally I got it, and I put my sermon down to turn to this man and began by asking him his name.

"Bernie," he said. "What's yours?"

"Brita."

"Brita," he said, "do you know what?"

"What, Bernie?" I said.

"Do you know that you and I are twins? Yes, you and I are twins."

A bit taken back I said, "Twins?"

I did not exactly see that there was a great similarity between us and obviously had been more tuned to the difference than similarity. Then he looked at me and said with a big smile, "Yes, twins. You see both have two eyes, two ears, and a mouth. That makes us twins."

Brita concludes, "Bernie was the one who shifted the perception for me to see that only those who see their unity with all, truly see. It is hard for me now to meet any stranger, to be in face of otherness, and not see Bernie's face reflected there." (Used by permission)

Brita Gill-Austern was the one who got a message that Sunday morning.

Especially in this Christmas season let us remember that the shepherds, the "forgotten ones," people of "low regard," were God's special, indeed God's honored, guests at Christmas. God cares for the poor. And so must we.

After all, we do have a lot in common.

Witnesses To Christmas:
The Angels

Luke 2:8-14

A little girl, previously an only child, was blessed with a baby brother. She was a good little girl, really. And she seemed thrilled to have a baby brother — at least most of the time. But she also sometimes seemed to her parents to be a little bit jealous of him. Sensing this, her parents told the little girl that the baby was a gift to their family from God. The baby had come to them *from* God. The little girl liked that idea.

Several days later she began pleading with her mother and father to be left alone with the baby. Still a bit worried about sibling rivalry, her parents were nervous about leaving her and the baby alone. But they realized there was an intercom in the baby's room, and that they could easily monitor what was going on in there, and rescue the baby if any real problems arose. So they relented.

The little girl went into the baby's room, closed the door tightly behind her, leaned over his crib and whispered in his ear, "Tell me about God. I'm starting to forget."

Like the little girl, every person, I believe, has something within herself or himself that longs to know God. We find something of the wonder and mystery of God in the freshness, the purity, and the innocence of babies. Especially in the Baby born in Bethlehem early on Christmas morning.

And around that Baby we find others who remind us of the wonder and mystery of God: a very special mother, Mary; a protective and loving father, Joseph; three kings guided by a star. And another very unique group of witnesses to Christmas, the angels in the Christmas story.

Angels appear throughout the Bible, from Genesis at the very beginning, to Revelation at the very end. They are found in scripture, all told, about a hundred times. Sometimes they guard and protect, as the angels protected Daniel from the lions in the lions' den (Daniel 6:22). Sometimes angels warn, as the angel warned Joseph in his dreams (Matthew 2:13). Sometimes they set people free from unjustified trouble, as the angel released Peter from prison (Acts 12:7). Sometimes they comfort, as angels comforted Jesus in the desert (Matthew 4:11). Sometimes angels wrestle with us, as an angel wrestled with Jacob all night (Genesis 32:24).

But whatever they do, throughout scripture, angels are depicted as being God's messengers. In ancient Greek, the word for "messenger" is actually *angelos*.

So if angels come to us from God, and if they bring messages to us from God, what are they saying? The message I get most clearly from the angels in the Christmas story is "Be not afraid." Every time the angels speak around Christmas, they say "Be not afraid!"

That's the first thing the angels say to the shepherds out in the fields: "Be not afraid, for behold, I bring you good tidings of great joy!" (Matthew 8:10 RSV). That's what Gabriel says to Mary, "Be not afraid, Mary! You have found favor with God!" (Luke 1:30 RSV). It's what the angel says to Joseph in his dreams, "Joseph, son of David, be not be afraid to take Mary as your wife" (Matthew 1:20b RSV).

"Be not afraid!" It's amazing to me that the angels say this to Mary, a teenage girl, who is pregnant without a husband.

To Joseph, a man who thinks the woman he loves has betrayed him. And to the shepherds, to a group of men, religious and social outcasts, living in poverty!

Still, the angel's message is consistent: "Be not afraid! Be not afraid! Be not afraid! Trust in God. Things may look bad. But God is good. And God can take the most difficult circumstances and turn them around!"

Charlie Shedd is a Presbyterian minister, now retired, and a best-selling author. In a recent book, *Brush Of An Angel's Wings* (Guideposts), he writes about a very difficult situation he once faced early in his career. When he was just out of theological school, doctors discovered that Charlie Shedd had a tumor on his larynx.

They couldn't tell at that time whether the tumor was malignant or not. His doctors felt they needed to operate, and right away. They told Charlie Shedd that during the operation, they might discover they would have to remove his larynx. If that happened, he would lose his voice. They told him also that even if they didn't remove his larynx, the operation might damage his vocal cords and cost him his speech.

Now Charlie Shedd had just completed four years of college, followed by three years of theological school. He was still in debt for his schooling. Even more importantly, he really wanted to be a teacher and preacher. He felt it was his vocation, his calling. He was terrified by the thought that he might lose his voice.

He writes that, on the way to the hospital in Omaha, his wife Martha reminded him of Psalm 34 and encouraged him to recite it. He did: "I sought the Lord and he heard me and delivered me from all my fears" (v. 4). But it didn't help. He was still afraid.

Turns out, he didn't lose his voice. At least, not permanently. The tumor was not malignant. But the surgery was deep and his larynx was damaged. Over the next several years, Charlie Shedd would lose his voice completely, from time to time, and have to rest it. That meant remaining absolutely silent for up to three months. Three months at a time without talking! Difficult for anyone. Nearly impossible for a preacher! But he did it.

During those weeks of silence, when his future was still unclear, Charlie Shedd would retire to his woodshed. Working in wood made him feel good. It took his mind off his troubles. He designed furniture. Some of his designs were good. He sold one to *Popular Mechanics* and got a much-needed check. This started Charlie Shedd to thinking that just maybe he could write.

He studied magazines and tried to discover what might interest publishers. Over the next few years, while his larynx was healing, Charlie Shedd wrote 55 articles for magazines. He averaged eleven rejections each. But he was persistent. He also wrote two best-selling books. He found himself launched on an unexpected new career as a writer.

To date, Charlie Shedd has authored over 35 books. He continues to write. He has also found his voice and lectures and preaches a lot. From his royalties and fees he has established a foundation that provides farm animals to poor people in the Philippines, Thailand, Korea, Zaire, Nigeria, India, and Haiti, and that supports a school for the developmentally challenged in Virginia.

He writes, "Thank you, Heavenly Father, for the way you can take a tumor on the larynx and turn it into a writing career. Thank you for the way you can take a writing career and turn that into missions" (p. 161). Over the years, Charlie Shedd learned to trust the message of the Christmas angels: "Be not afraid! Be not afraid! Be not afraid!" Things may look bad. But God is good. And God has surprising ways of turning things around.

That kind of expectant hopefulness is an essential part of the Christmas message. For the Baby born in Bethlehem, so innocent and pure, coming to us from God — indeed, God's Self — knew unjustified suffering and trouble his whole life long. Steve Lovejoy, our church sexton, when he lived out in the countryside of Vermont, used to keep cattle and sheep. He kept them out in a little stable in the middle of a big field. Steve built a big cross over the peak of the stable and lit it with white lights at Christmas time. People would stop along the roadside to take pictures of the stable with the cross. There's a wisdom there: from the very moment of his birth, Jesus lived in the shadow of the cross.

His childhood was lived out in that same shadow. There's a famous painting of the child Jesus running from the carpenter's shop with outstretched arms toward Mary, his mother. The sun, shining on his outstretched arms, makes the shadow of the cross behind the boy.

In adulthood Jesus headed resolutely toward Jerusalem and toward incredible suffering. On the night before he died, knowing full well what lay ahead of him the next morning, he went into the Garden of Gethsemane with eleven of his disciples to pray. He left eight by the gate and took three with him farther into the Garden. Then, at the end, he went off under the olive trees alone, to fight the hardest battle of his life.

In an agony of spirit, after having prayed that this cup might pass from him, Jesus prepared to receive it, to drink every bit of it.

And an angel came from God and strengthened him (Luke 22:43). Maybe the angel said, "Be not afraid."

I don't know whether *you* personally believe in angels or not. According to a *Time* magazine poll, 69 percent of Americans do (December 27, 1993). But then, 25 percent of Americans do not. And the other six percent apparently aren't sure. I don't know whether you believe in angels or not, but I hope you believe that there are spiritual realities beyond our comprehension. I hope you believe that there is a Power working in your life, and throughout creation, for the good. I hope you believe that sometimes things might look awful. But that God can use even the worst tragedy, God can use even the worst injustice, God can use even a cross, and turn it to good.

I hope this Christmas you hear the angels' message, "Be not afraid! Be not afraid! Be not afraid!" And can take it to heart.

Witnesses to Christmas: The Animals

Isaiah 11:6-9; Mark 13:32-37

Recently I ran across a lovely old English Christmas ballad titled "The Storke." This ballad was found written in the flyleaf of a prayerbook that belonged to Edward the Sixth, a boy king who died at age fifteen. Edward must have liked this poem. The old ballad tells the story of a stork on Christmas Eve in the Holy Land. On learning that Jesus was born in Bethlehem, the stork leaves her brood with food and flies to the manger. When she arrives, she weeps to see the Son of God laid in such a rude, rough cradle. The stork reaches down with her long neck and plucks the down from her breast to make a warm, soft nest for the baby. The Baby Jesus, now more comfortable, turns in the stork's direction, and smiles. Since then, says the old ballad, the stork is always welcome in every town and village and is known throughout the world as the "friend of babies."

It's a nice old story, one of many that links animals to Christmas. There are a great many animal/Christmas connections, aren't there, from that famous painting of Edward Hicks, *The Peaceable Kingdom*, to Dasher, Dancer, Prancer, and Vixen, Comet, Cupid, Donder and Blitzen, and the "most famous reindeer of all," pulling Santa's sled.

Animals and Christmas seem to go together. So it's interesting to me that no animals are mentioned anywhere in Matthew or Luke's accounts of the birth of Jesus, except sheep. And Luke says that the shepherds left their flocks out in the fields. It was Saint Francis of Assisi, that great lover of animals, who added the ox, donkey, and sheep to our traditional crèche set when he created the first living crèche back in 1224.

Still we can guess that, if Jesus was born in a stable and laid in a manger — a feeding trough for cows — there were animals there. Probably oxen, cows, donkeys, chickens, maybe a few dogs and

71

cats. Everything except pigs — the Jews didn't eat pork and didn't keep pigs.

So along with Mary and Joseph and the shepherds and the angels and the Wise Men, the animals were also witnesses to Christmas. The presence of the animals says something. But what?

That's a theological question. And I'd like you folks to be thinking theologically this morning. That's no big deal, really. After all, the little girl was asking a theological question when she wrote in a letter to God: "Dear God, do animals use you, too? Or is there someone else for them? (Signed) Nancy."

The word "theology" means "God talk" in Greek. I'd like you to be "God talkers" today. A little bit later, I'm going to ask you, "How do animals witness to God for you?" Be thinking about that, please.

But first, let me offer a few roughed-out thoughts of my own, about God and Christ and human beings and animals. One thing I think of when I think of the Son of God being born among the animals is that this is a reminder of the interconnectedness of life. Or, as one biologist, Elisabet Sahtouris, has put it, of the "embeddedness" of life.

Jesus could have been born anywhere: in a house, in a tent, in a palace, in the inn. The innkeeper could have said to Mary and Joseph, "You're in luck! We just had a cancellation!"

But no! The story says Jesus was born in a stable, out behind the inn. As far as we know, there were no other people there, except his parents.

Was that an accident? Or is it a message? Maybe a message about God's love for all living things. Maybe a reminder of that wonderful image from Isaiah: "The wolf shall dwell with the lamb, and the leopard shall lie down with the kid, and the calf and the lion and the fatling together, and a little child shall lead them" (v. 6 RSV). The child who makes peace in all of creation is Jesus, born among the animals.

And I also wonder, is there a special connection between Christ and the animals? Is Christ to be found, not only in human beings, but also in animals, too? It says in the first chapter of the Gospel of John: "All things were made through [Christ], and without him was not anything made that was made (1:3 RSV). Earlier generations of Christians, living closer to nature, saw Christ in lots of living things.

There's a wonderful, strange book in our church library titled *The Bestiary of Christ* (Arkana Books). It's by a French scholar named Louis Charbonneau-Lassay. This book is his collection of Christian symbolism related to animals. Animals have often been used as symbols of Christ.

Some of the animal symbols for Jesus are well-known: the Lamb of God (John 1:29), the Lion of Judah (Revelation 5:5). And in the early Church, one of the common symbols for Jesus was the fish. The letters of the word "fish" in Greek was an acrostic for "Jesus Christ, Son of God, Savior."

But Jesus has also been symbolized as many other animals. Like a bee. The bee, "dying" in winter, "rising" in the spring, was seen as a symbol of resurrection. Or a pelican. The ancients believed the pelican wounded itself with its beak to bring forth blood to revive its young. Christ revives us with his blood. Sometimes Jesus was portrayed as an eagle. Eagles kill snakes, and the snake is a symbol for Satan. Or as a stag, a male deer, because the stag is always on watch. In the early Church in Rome, Jesus was even symbolized by a praying mantis, because Jesus was constantly praying!

Well, why not? As Walt Whitman put it, "A mouse is miracle enough to stagger [many millions] of infidels." Can't the animals represent Christ to us?

And if Christ was born among the animals and might be found in the animals, what does that mean for the way we treat the animals? Lincoln once said that you can tell a lot about a man's religion by the way he treats his dog or cat (paraphrase). What does it say about our religion — or lack of religion — the way we've treated the other living things?

We love our pets! And why not? They love us. As G. K. Chesterton put it, "Every man is a god — in the eyes of his dog. Hence the popularity of dogs!" But we haven't done so well with the rest of creation.

Every one of us average Americans create, on average, more than twice our body weight in garbage and pollution daily. Due to overfishing and pollution, fish stocks are depleted just off of Cape Cod, an area once so rich in fish that they named it after the cod. Sea turtles with huge tumors growing on their bodies, caused by pollution, wash up on our shores. United Nations organizations estimate that by the year 2,000 we human beings will have driven to extinction a million other species.

Human beings are actually the most dangerous animals on this planet. Mark Twain, who loved cats, once wrote that if someone were to crossbreed a cat and a human being, the human being would be improved. But the cat would be diminished!

There's an image in Romans, chapter 8, that I like. Paul writes that all creation is "groaning," groaning in travail, waiting with "eager longing" to be set free from its "bondage to decay." All creation is waiting for the release of the sons and daughters of God, says Romans (8:19-22 RSV). All creation is waiting for us to wake up!

The other day I saw a bumper sticker with a picture of a whale on it. The whale was spouting a saying: Save the humans! It's not just the whales but the whole world that needs to be saved from us. And we from ourselves.

We need to do work on the theology for a small planet. I like what some churches are doing: blessing the animals. Hal Cooper and the Council of Churches do this every year at the West Yarmouth Congregational Church. Some years they have blessed over two hundred pets: dogs, cats, rats, birds, fish, gerbils, goats, ponies, a Vietnamese pig.

I read somewhere that they do the same at the Cathedral Church of St. John the Divine in Morningside Heights. Only there they bring the circus animals into the sanctuary to be blessed — including the elephants. They bless "all creatures great and small," including, one year, a beaker of algae.

Blessing algae? Silly? Maybe. Or maybe not. Maybe that's a first, small step in recognizing our interconnectedness with all of life. "[God] hath put all things under (our) feet ... the birds of the air, and the fish of the sea, whatever passes along the paths of the sea" (Psalm 8:8 RSV). Including the algae. "All things were made through him, and without him was not anything made that was made" (John 1-3 RSV). Including the algae.

I think about the servants in the parable in Mark. The Master left them temporarily in charge of his property. The Master went away for a while. Meanwhile he expected his servants to take good care of his property. And the Master wasn't accepting any excuses. He was coming back. He expected them alert and awake (Mark 13:32-37).

We are accountable to God for God's creation. We are accountable to God for the health of this planet. We are accountable to God for what happens to our world. And we can no longer say we are asleep to the environmental crisis. That's no excuse.

That, I think, is also part of the message of Christmas. Jesus was born among the animals. God loves them and came to save them, too. "For God so loved the world," it says, "for God so loved the world," and everything in it, "that he gave his only Son" (John 3:16a RSV).

There isn't "somebody else" for the animals. Christ is among them, and in them, and for them. And we are held accountable as God's stewards.

That's the message I get from the animals at Christmas. What about you? What do the animals say to *you* about God?

Witnesses To Christmas:
The Wise Men

Matthew 2:1-12

"'Tis the week after Christmas; 'Tis the week after Christmas, and all through the house, not a package was still wrapped, not even a blouse. The stockings were picked up from the chimney where they fell. But, the children were fighting and starting to yell. Yes, fighting and yelling and shouting their dreads. The sugar they've eaten has gone to their heads! The excitement of New Year's is finally past. The bowl games are over. Back to normal, at last!"

It does seem as if the holidays are over, doesn't it? But, technically speaking, we're still in the Christmas season, until the Twelfth Day of Christmas, which is tomorrow. So there is still time to put the Wise Men in the crèche set (if there's any room for them!) and talk about them. On this, the Sunday closest to Epiphany, we generally think about the "Three Kings." For, tradition says it was on Epiphany that they arrived.

And, we all know the story of the Three Kings, don't we? Or, do we? Actually, the Bible doesn't exactly say that there were three. We get the idea of three from the mention of three gifts. Nor does the Bible actually say they were "kings," either. "Wise Men" is what these travelers are called.

One *woman* has said that these guys were "wise" simply because, unlike most men she knew, *they* were at least willing to stop and ask for directions! They were wise about that! But they were wise in other ways, too. They were probably very wise about the stars. The Magi were probably court astrologers from ancient Persia, which is modern-day Iraq. They might have been Zoroastrians, Medes, Persians, Arabs, or even Jews.

What they did for a living was to observe and study the sky. Then they interpreted the signs of the night sky for royal patrons. In those days, court astrologers were powerful people. The root for the word "magi" has the same root as the English word, "magic."

The magi were believed to have magical powers. They were sophisticated, by the standards of their day, well-educated, and important individuals, accustomed to giving advice to royalty. They were important enough for King Herod, himself, known as "Herod the Great," to give them an audience right off.

In addition to being students of the stars, the Wise Men were also honest seekers. Think about what they went through to follow that star! They left their homes and families to go on a long and dangerous journey. They set off without knowing exactly where they would end up. Or how long they might be gone.

I wonder: how did they explain this trip to their wives? I can hear their wives, Mrs. Gaspar, Mrs. Melchoir, and Mrs. Balthshasar now. Mrs. Gaspar says, "You say you're going to follow a what?" Mrs. Melchior says, "And you can't tell us how long you'll be gone?!" Mrs. Balthshasar says, "And you're going off with Gaspar and Melchoir?! You know those two are always trouble! And besides, you promised that, after the first of the year, you'd be home every night for supper!"

Then there were the rigors of the journey itself. Through the burning sands and freezing nights of the Arabian desert, they followed the star. Rocking back and forth on the backs of their camels, they followed the star. Through sandstorms and windstorms, in danger of getting lost, in danger of attack by robbers, they followed the star. There must have been times when the light of that star seemed very dim. And they still weren't exactly sure where they were going. But they still faithfully followed the star.

Finally, they arrive at Jerusalem, the capital city, thinking that their long journey must be over. They were expecting a big celebration, torches lit, trumpets blaring, crowds dancing in the streets, rejoicing at the birth of a King. But not a soul is stirring. Even the birth of a puppy would have caused more excitement in Jerusalem than the birth of Jesus (Luther). After a brief visit with King Herod, the Wise Men push on.

They arrive at Bethlehem. And what do they find there? Just a dusty village. No royal palace, no royal entourage, no royal family. Just a couple of poor peasants in a stable out behind the inn with a little baby cradled in a manger.

What do you think the Wise Men thought and felt? Matthew says that "when they saw that the star had stopped, they were overwhelmed with joy" (2:10 NRSV). And why not? The star had stopped. Their long and dangerous journey seemed to be over. They could climb off the camels. No more saddle sores, for a while!

But how do you think they felt when they saw what they did? How would you have felt? All that way to see a peasant baby laid in the straw in a feeding trough for cattle, surrounded by the smells and manure of the animals? How do you think they might have felt? Puzzled? Confused? Disappointed? Maybe a little let down? We'll never know. But we can well imagine.

Still, in faith, the Wise Men knelt down and worshiped. They laid their expensive gifts of gold, frankincense, and myrrh at the unknown baby's feet.

What are these Wise Men witness to? To me, they are witnesses to the riskiness of faith. We might well prefer a faith that is safe. C. S. Lewis speaks for a lot of us when he writes: "I am a safety-first creature. I am cautious and careful ... But," he continues, "if I am sure of anything, I am sure that Jesus' teaching was never meant to confirm my preference for safe investments and limited liabilities." He concludes, in faith there is no "safe investment ... Love anything and your heart will certainly be wrung [out] and possibly be broken" (*The Four Loves*, Harcourt Brace Jovanovich, pp. 168-169).

Speaking of our desire for a comfortable, risk-free faith, Wilbur Rees puts it another way: "I would like to buy $3.00 worth of God, please. Not enough [God] to explode my soul, or disturb my sleep ... just enough [God] to equal a cup of warm milk, or a snooze in the sunshine. I don't want enough [God] ... to make me love a Black man or pick beets with a migrant worker. No, I want ecstasy and not transformation. I want the warmth of the womb, not a new birth. I want a pound of Eternal in a paper bag. I would like to buy just $3.00 worth of God, please" (quoted by Tim Hansel in *When I Relax I Feel Guilty*, David C. Cook Publishing Co., p. 49).

It's very human to want a God who provides us with a lot of comfort, but little challenge. But we can't just buy "$3.00 worth of God." We've got to invest ourselves in the journey of faith. The journey has to mean something to us, and cost us something, as it did the Wise Men.

For it is often only after we travel through the wilderness of bewilderment, following the sometimes dim light in the darkness, and maybe even getting lost, but pushing on, that we can get wise to God's Surprise. The surprise is that the God we are seeking so hard is already seeking us. That the God we are looking for "out there" is already here and near.

The Wise Men sought God in the stars. They found God in a Baby. God reaches out to us in the simplest of things: in a Baby in a manger. In a table set with bread and wine.

The Dutch Benedictines have a rule that they teach their initiates. The rule concludes, "So never let yourselves lose heart, but go on seeking God in everything, [and] everybody ... they are all places that you will finally meet [the One who is seeking you]."

The three Wise Men took the risk of faith — and discovered Emmanuel, "God with us."

Maybe that's why we call them "wise."

Don't Forget The Child!

Micah 5:2-5a; Luke 1:46-55

Most of us are familiar with the blockbuster movies, *Home Alone* and *Home Alone 2: Lost In New York*. They played around Christmas time for two consecutive years. In *Home Alone*, little nine-year-old Kevin is accidentally left behind in the Chicago suburbs while his family flies off for a Christmas vacation in Paris. In its sequel, Kevin mistakenly boards a plane for New York City while the rest of his family heads off to Florida.

Several recent real-life cases of child neglect have made the concept of leaving young children home alone a whole lot less funny. Remember the Chicago couple who left *their* nine-year-old to take care of herself *and* her four-year-old sister, while they went off on vacation for nine days to Mexico?

I'd like to see Kevin's parents have to explain a few things to a judge: explain why *they're* not guilty of child neglect! They seem like nice people. They take great vacations. But especially around Christmas, you *don't forget the child!*

But then, if we're honest with ourselves, we might have to admit that sometimes we can be guilty of "child neglecting" around Christmas. Not neglecting our own children or grandchildren, of course. They have their ways of not letting us forget them, especially around Christmas!

No, the Child we sometimes "ignore," "overlook," "leave behind," "neglect" is God's Son. For many of us, this Christmas season, and especially this last week of Advent, is a frightfully busy time: the biggest shopping days of the year, one of the busiest travel periods of the year, a time when many businesses hope to make, often *need to* make, up to 45 percent of their annual profits. For many, it's a time of mounting celebrations and office parties, a time of writing out cards, wrapping gifts, hanging lights, decorating trees, baking brownies. Sometimes we get so absorbed in preparing for Christmas that we forget the Reason for the Season. One of our church members puts it well. In the midst of all the frantic activity in this season, our Christmas can become "Xmas," with the Christ "X-ed" out.

But then, it's often been easy to overlook the Child. He was, after all, largely ignored, overlooked, and neglected by the world on that first Christmas. "He was in the world, and the world was made through him, yet the world knew him not. He came to his own home, and his own people received him not" (John 1:10-11 RSV). You see, during the period when Christ was born, the world's attention was focused, not on Bethlehem, but on Rome.

"All roads lead to Rome." Rome was where everything important was happening. The Roman Empire was the greatest political and economic creation of the Ancient World. It was huge, stretching from the Atlantic Ocean on the west, to the Euphrates on the east. It stretched, at that time, as far south as the Sahara Desert and as far north as the Danube. And all this massive empire was ruled by one man. Caesar Augustus was his name.

Tucked away in Caesar's mighty empire was a narrow strip of land along the Mediterranean known as Palestine, an impoverished, conquered territory that was considered a cultural backwater. Tucked into one corner of Palestine near the south, in a hilly region, was the little town of Bethlehem. Its name in Hebrew means "House of Bread." It was a village as plain and ordinary as a loaf of bread.

Now if someone had told Caesar Augustus, sitting in his palace in the capital, Rome, that history was about to be made by a Jewish baby being born in Bethlehem into a family headed by a hillbilly father, born to a teenage mother, he would have laughed. Caesar would not have known where Bethlehem was. It was too insignificant a spot to attract the attention of someone like him. Besides, Caesar would have contended that history is made, not by weak, defenseless babies, but by people like him. After all, hadn't he just ordered a census so that "all the world should be enrolled" (Luke 2:1 RSV) that was disrupting the entire world? Even if he had known about the birth of Jesus, Caesar Augustus, in his pomp and circumstance, would have considered it of no account. Caesar Augustus was among those who overlooked the Child.

Most of the people of his time ignored him. We may sometimes forget him. But God does not forget Jesus! Eight hundred years before Caesar Augustus, Micah, God's prophet, informed the world about how it would go. Micah spoke these words in the name of the Lord:

> *Bethlehem ... you are one of the smallest towns in Judah, but out of you will I bring a Ruler for Israel, whose family line goes back to ancient times. When he comes, he will rule his people with the strength that comes from the Lord and with the majesty of the Lord God himself. His people will live in safety because people all over the earth will acknowledge his greatness, and he will bring peace.*
> — Micah 5:2-5a (TEV)

Eight long centuries *before* Christ, the Lord God put his finger on little Bethlehem, the insignificant "House of Bread," and announced that this backwater village would be the birthplace of his Son. Caesar Augustus no doubt thought *he* was pretty clever ordering that census. But mighty Caesar was only a messenger boy, a minor character in the plot. Caesar, and the whole machinery of the Roman Empire, were merely God's instruments to get Mary and Joseph to travel from Nazareth to Bethlehem, a distance of eighty miles. God had a plan. God had never forgotten the Child!

You see, it's often what we consider insignificant that God considers important. And what we consider important that God considers insignificant. An impoverished land, a backwater village, a run-down stable, a teenage mother, a poor child's birth: we might overlook them. A mighty Caesar, an enormous palace, prestige, and power: we might be impressed. But God's values are often the reverse of this world's.

Mary, the mother of Jesus, was a woman who was humble, plain, and simple. But also obedient, insightful, and faithful. With

83

her simple faith, Mary understood a lot of the values of God. Mary praised God's ways in the Magnificat, a hymn that the early church attributed to her:

> *[God] has shown strength with his arm, he has scattered the proud (like Caesar Augustus) in the imagination of their hearts, he has put down the mighty from their thrones, and exalted those (like Mary) of low degree; he has filled the hungry with good things, and the rich he has sent empty away.*
>
> — Luke 1:51-53 (RSV)

Christmas is more than just a family holiday; more than just a winter-time celebration to "knock back" the dark and the cold; more than just an economic and social event; more than just an opportunity to play host to coworkers, neighbors, and friends (although it *is* all of these things, too!). It is the breaking into our world of God's long-awaited Messiah. It is God's overturning of the values of our world. It is the promise that, through this Child, this Christ, the *spiritually* hungry *and* the *physically* hungry *will be* fed. It is the miracle of the Incarnation, God becoming flesh and dwelling among us. It is the beginning of the ultimate act of love: God wanting so much to communicate with us, to share God's self with us, that God breaks into our world and becomes a human being. A human being who willingly dies for us on a Cross! It's the Light of God shining in our world's darkness, and overcoming the darkness.

You don't see all this if you only look at the birth of Christ with the eyes of Caesar, with the jaded eyes of the world. You have to look at Christmas with the eyes of Mary, the eyes of wondering faith.

I really hope you enjoy this Christmas! Go out and celebrate! Laugh and exchange gifts and eat too much, rejoice in life, thank God for family and friends, squeeze your grandchildren until they think they'll burst! Like any loving Parent, God is happy when God's children are happy. God rejoices in our holiday joy.

But don't forget, Christmas is not just something passing. It's something radical. It's the bursting of God into our world. It's the overturning of the values of this world. It's the fulfillment of prophecy and God's plan which has unfolded since the beginning of Creation. Let it be a time of awe and reverence and wonderment, of inviting the Child into your heart.

Do it all! Really celebrate Christmas! We need that light in the darkness. But in the midst of it all, don't forget the Child!

Yes, Virginia, There Is A Savior!

Isaiah 35:1-7; Luke 1:46-55

Over 100 years ago now, in 1897, there was an exchange of letters which has become a part of American folklore. It started when eight-year-old Virginia O'Hanlon of New York City wrote this letter to the editor of *The New York Sun*.

"Dear Editor," wrote Virginia, "I am eight years old. Some of my little friends say there is no Santa Claus. Papa says, 'If you see it in *The Sun*, it's so.' Please tell me the truth. Is there a Santa Claus?"

Sun Editor Frank Church (don't you *love* that name, "Frank Church"?) published this famous response. I'll read it in part: " ... Yes, Virginia, there *is* a Santa Claus. He exists as certainly as love, and generosity and devotion exist, and you know that they abound and give your life its highest beauty and joy." Editor Frank Church continued, "Alas! How dreary would be the world if there were no Santa Claus! It would be as dreary as if there were no Virginias. There would be no childlike faith, then, no poetry, no romance to make more tolerable this existence. We should have no enjoyment, except in sense and sight. The eternal light with which childhood fills the world would be extinguished ... No Santa Claus? Thank God he lives and he lives forever. A thousand years from now, Virginia, nay, ten times ten thousand years from now, he will continue to make glad the heart of childhood."

Frank Church is right! There *is* a Santa Claus! Of course, all that business about a bearded, jolly fat man in a red suit with eight tiny reindeer isn't *literally* true! (And, I hope, by revealing that, I haven't spoiled anyone's Christmas!) But you could say that there *is* evidence of a certain "Santa Claus" spirit.

Consider these headlines from *The Register*, our local weekly paper: "Santa Arrives at [Salvation] Army Bearing Gifts for Needy: Tech Students Donate Clothing"; "Churches Seek Donations for the Needy"; "Army to Help Family with No Tree"; "Scargo Students Provide Canned Goods for Needy"; and so on. This time of year especially, our hearts are open for caring, and our hands are open for sharing. There *is* a Santa!

But let's remember again who the original Saint Nicholas was. He was a real person who lived in Asia Minor (some say Turkey) around the year 300 A.D. His parents were wealthy. Nicholas himself was a person of great faith, who wanted to live in imitation of Christ. So Nicholas spent a fair amount of his family fortune feeding the needy. Seeking to draw no attention to himself, Nicholas did his gift-giving at night, slipping gold coins under the doors of the poorest homes. He eventually became a monk and later a bishop, the youngest bishop in the history of the early Church. Like many other early Christians, Nicholas was imprisoned and tortured for his beliefs. Saint Nicholas represents the spirit of unselfish giving that grows not out of a fuzzy sentimentality, but out of gratitude for our Salvation in Jesus Christ.

There *is* a Santa because there is a *Savior*. The name "Jesus" actually means "to save." And we *need* to be saved. We *all* need to be saved because *all* of us get "stuck" in sin.

In his book, *Finding Hope When God Seems Silent*, Ben Patterson provides a dramatic illustration of how a person's sin can lead to a kind of "stuckness." (Reported by Gordon MacDonald in "Repentance," *Preaching Today*, tape no. 121.) Patterson writes about a climbing trip he took with three companions to Mount Lyell, the highest peak in Yosemite National Park. Two of the climbers were experienced. Patterson and one other man were not. Patterson explains the situation which developed like this: "The climb to the top and back was to take the better part of a day due, in large part, to the difficulty of the glacier that one must cross to get to the top ... As the hours passed, and we trudged up the glacier, the two [experienced climbers] opened up a wide gap between me and my less-experienced companion. Being competitive by nature, I began to look for short cuts I might be able to take to beat them to the top. I thought I saw one to the right of an outcropping of rock — so I went up, deaf to the protests of my companions."

He continues, "Thirty minutes later I was trapped in a cul-de-sac of rock atop the Lysell Glacier, looking down several hundred feet of a sheer drop of ice, pitched at a 45-degree angle ... I was only ten feet from the safety of a rock. But one little slip and I wouldn't stop sliding until I landed in the valley floor ... I was stuck and I was scared."

Every one of us has found ourselves in situations like that: maybe not *literally* trapped on the side of a glacier, but figuratively "stuck," scared, trapped because of our own stupidity and sin, desperately seeking someone to rescue us from the trouble and pain we have created for ourselves.

No wonder there is such a mournful quality to our Advent hymns! "O come, O come, Emmanuel, and ransom captive Israel," ("We feel like captives, and we're awaiting Someone to come to our rescue!"); "Watchman, tell us of the night" ("We're struggling in the darkness. Is there hope?"). During Advent especially we concentrate on the limitations of our human condition, on our brokenness and creation's brokenness, on our weakness, on our "stuckness," on how much we need Someone who will come to our help.

Back to Bob Patterson, hanging by a thread on that cliff. He writes, "It took an hour for my experienced climbing friends to find me. Standing on the rock I wanted to reach, one of them leaned out and used an ice ax to chip two little footsteps in the glacier. Then he gave me the following instructions: 'Ben, you must step out from where you are and put your foot where the first foothold is. Without a moment's hesitation swing your other foot across and land it in the next step. [Then] ... reach out and I will take your hand, and I will pull you to safety ...'"

The more experienced climber continued, "But listen carefully: as you step across, *don't* lean into the mountain! If anything, lean out a bit. Otherwise, your feet could fly out from under you and you will start sliding down."

His friend was asking Patterson, stuck on a cliff, to let go for just an instant and to trust that his friend could and would save him. Save him from a plunge down the glacier to certain death. His friend was asking him to trust him so completely that Patterson would even lean back away from the seeming safety and security of the mountain for a just moment so his friend could reach down and grab him and pull him up.

Patterson writes: "I looked at [my friend] real hard ... for a moment, based solely on what I believed to be true about the good will and good sense of my friend, I decided ... to [step out and lean out and trust completely in him]. It took less than two seconds to find out if my faith was well founded. It was." Patterson was saved.

So also are *we* saved when *we* are stuck in sin, if *we* recognize our stuckness, and put our trust in the One who *is* above us and reaching down to save us. That's Jesus. And when we really realize that we *have* been saved from sin, from that terrible plunge to disaster; in gratitude, in *relief*, we just might be moved to extend a hand to someone else. *That's* what the "Christmas Spirit" is all about: one grateful, saved sinner reaching out to other people, giving because he has already received, as Saint Nicholas gave so willingly and so generously long ago. We give at Christmas because we recognize the greater gift that God has given us.

I discovered something interesting about Frank Church's response to little Virginia. Suppose we were to substitute the name of Santa Claus for the name of Jesus. Consider how it reads:

Yes, Virginia, there is a Savior. He exists as certainly as love and devotion exist ... Alas! How dreary would be the world if there were no Jesus! ... There would be no childlike faith then ... to make tolerable this existence. We should have no enjoyment, except in sense and sight. The eternal light with which childhood fills the world would be extinguished ... No Jesus Christ? Thank God he lives and he lives forever. A thousand years from now, Virginia, nay, ten times ten thousand years from now, Jesus will continue to make glad [our] hearts.

A world without a Savior is dreary and dangerous. In a world without a Savior, all of us will eventually get stuck. Without a Savior to rescue us, all of us eventually will fall.

But with a Savior, there is hope.

Yes, Virginia, there *is* a Santa, a spirit of caring and sharing especially evident around Christmas. But there is a Santa because there is a Savior, who provides those who believe in him with a reason to give and live. My hope for all of us is that we can recognize our stuckness and reach up to the one who is reaching down to help us. Then, in gratitude and thanksgiving, that we might reach out a hand of help to others, not just in the Christmas season but for as long as we live.

The Best Christmas Pageant Ever

Luke 2:1-20

What would *you* say is "The Best Christmas Pageant *Ever*"?

Some say *The Glory of Christmas*, held at the Crystal Cathedral in Garden Grove, California, for the last eighteen years, is best. This is from a recent press release:

"The Crystal Cathedral's *Glory of Christmas* contains a splendor, scale and theatricality that few productions anywhere can ... equal ... singled out by the *Today Show*, *Good Morning America* [and] *Entertainment Tonight* ... the ... *Glory of Christmas* is ... recognized nationwide ... Reminiscent of such stage extravaganzas as *Phantom of the Opera* and ... *Beauty and the Beast* ..." The musical score was recorded by members of the London Symphony Orchestra.

The press release continues, "Zeon 'Super Trooper' spot lights — developed (by the military) for long distance surveillance" spotlight the 124-foot wide, 80-foot high stage, "one of the largest indoor sets in the world." A 2,000-watt light "provides the effect of the (Star of Bethlehem) shining down on the Christ Child through the Cathedral's 90-foot doors."

There are over 200 performers, plus horses, goats, donkeys, sheep, and camels. Eight actors dressed as angels fly simultaneously over the audience — suspended on cables hung nine stories in the air. *The Glory of Christmas* is shown three times a day, except Christmas Eve and Christmas. The press release concludes, "VISA, MasterCard and American Express accepted."

Some statistics! Some show! I'm sure *The Glory of Christmas* is spectacular! But, is it the *best* Christmas pageant *ever*?

Others think the best Christmas pageant is the one described in Barbara Robinson's book, *The Best Christmas Pageant Ever*. Maybe you remember it. Ralph, Imogene, Leroy, Claude, Ollie, and Gladys Herdman, "six skinny, stringy-haired kids all alike except for being different sizes and having different black-and-blue spots where they had clonked each other" grab all the major roles in a small church's Christmas play. The Herdmans are described as: "absolutely the worst kids in the history of the world." They "lied and stole and smoked cigars (even the girls) and talked dirty and hit little kids and cussed their teachers and took the name of the Lord in vain and set fire to Fred Shoemaker's old broken-down toolhouse" (*The Best Christmas Pageant Ever*, HarperCollins Publishers, p. 1).

The Herdmans terrorize the other children at church, drink the communion grape juice, steal pennies from the birthday bank, and are accused of setting the church on fire. Actually, that last part *wasn't* true. It was only Imogene Herdman smoking a cigar in the ladies room. However, the Herdmans *do* ruin the applesauce cake for the potluck supper. *And* get Reverend Hopkins so upset he forgets how he's dressed. So he rushes over to the church in his pajamas and bathrobe, in front of the Ladies Aid Society.

Still, it turns out to be a wonderful pageant. The wild Herdmans are tamed by the story of the Baby Jesus. The congregation is touched. Barbara Robinson's book *is* a classic. But, *is* it "The Best Christmas Pageant *Ever*"?

Certainly the most *ambitious* pageant *this church* has ever attempted is "The Bethlehem Marketplace" this morning. Our CE Director, Ginnie Haskell, is the greatest director since Cecil B. DeMille. Church School Hall downstairs has been transformed into ancient Bethlehem. There's a synagogue, complete with bearded rabbi, carpentry, weaving, and pottery shops, food stalls, the village well, the "No Room Inn" and, of course, a stable.

The actors — forty splendidly costumed children and adults, and one sheep named Rachael — play craftspeople, townspeople, moneychangers, census takers, lepers, centurions, dancers, shepherds, Mary and Joseph — and a sheep. All the sights, sounds, and smells of Bethlehem on the night Jesus was born are there in the air. It's magic. Our children will remember The Bethlehem Marketplace for decades. But, is this the best Christmas pageant *ever*? What makes a Christmas pageant great?

We'll get back to that question in a bit. But first a story: for years I kept fresh-water tropical fish in my office at my previous church in West Springfield. The tank and fish actually started off in the parsonage next door. It was a fair amount of work — testing the ph, cleaning the tank, feeding the fish, treating their diseases. The fish were expensive. Their equipment was expensive.

Still, I loved and cared for those little creatures. I learned their names. I learned their needs. Each one was precious to me.

Believe it or not, I even suffered for my fish. I got a rare bacterial infection while cleaning out the tank. My hand swelled up. A line of bright red nodules ran up my arm. It wasn't painful. But it was very scary. It took my local doctor plus two specialists to figure out what I had.

Summer approached. We were going away on a month's vacation. The church sexton said he would care for my fish. But first I had to move them to my office next door. It wasn't far. I figured I could carry the tank *with* the fish in it — if I drained out about half the water.

I walked very slowly and carefully. But as I walked, the water inside the tank started to slosh from side to side. The poor fish! They were trapped in a tidal wave of water! It must have seemed to them like their little world was about to end!

When I stopped moving, the water settled, and most of the fish adjusted. Except for the catfish. His eyes bugged out. He turned from a light pink to a ghostly white. And thereafter, it seemed every time I came into my office, the catfish immediately hid in the castle. He wouldn't come out again until I left.

I imagine to that catfish, I was a terrible, all-powerful god, a Supreme Demon Monster that could pick up his entire world and throw it into utter chaos. I'd like to think my IQ is about 6,000 times that of a catfish. I know my experience is vastly greater. I can hop on a plane and fly to Europe. He was trapped in a ten-gallon tank. I might live to be a hundred. He would be lucky if he lived to be two. The gap between us was immense, enormous, overwhelming. How could I communicate my love to something so simple, weak, and small? How could I ever get that catfish to trust me again?

I thought: maybe if I kept all my human wisdom and experience, but became a catfish, maybe then I could reach him. Maybe if I gave up everything, and entered his dark, smelly, murky, bottom-dwelling, tank scavenger existence, maybe if I took upon myself the risks of his short, limited life, maybe then we could communicate, and he would understand.

Well, I liked my fish! But never that much! Even if such a metamorphosis were possible, I wouldn't do it. None of us would. *But here's the point!* A human being choosing to become a catfish is nothing ... nothing ... nothing ... compared to the risk and sacrifice of God choosing to become a human being!

We tend to think bigger and bigger is better, don't we? Angels soaring nine stories in the air over the Crystal Cathedral; ninety foot doors; a 2,000 watt spotlight; a cast of 200; the world's largest indoor stage. To us, size and scale and splendor are impressive.

But the real mystery and wonder of Christmas is the Creator of the universe becoming smaller and smaller and smaller. It's God's Son, giving up the wonders and joys of heaven, and his intimate closeness to God, and coming down, down, down. It's the Wonderful Counselor, Mighty God, Everlasting Father, Prince of Peace becoming a single fertilized egg, almost too tiny to be seen, growing in the womb of an unmarried Jewish teenager. It's the Alpha and Omega, the Beginning and End, the Ancient of Days, emerging as a Baby who couldn't speak or feed himself or change his own diapers. It's the Almighty, who moves kings and empires like pawns on a chessboard, lying in a cow's feeding trough in a smelly stable on a bed of straw.

Why? Maybe that was the only way God could communicate with us — by coming down to our level, by taking on God's Self the limitations and humiliations of being a human being. God reached out to us by "getting into the tank with us" so that we could see clearly the depth and power and extent of God's love.

When we really grasp the wonder of Christmas, Emmanuel, God with us, it *can* change us. It changed the Herdmans in Barbara Robinson's wonderful story. Remember the Herdmans, "absolutely the worst kids in the history of the world," who "lied and stole and smoked cigars (even the girls) and talked dirty and hit little kids and cussed their teachers and took the name of the Lord in vain" and terrorized every child in the Christmas play?

At the end of the Christmas pageant, mean Imogene Herdman was crying. Robinson writes: "In the candlelight her face was all shiny with tears, and she didn't even bother to wipe them away. She just sat there — awful old Imogene — crying and crying and crying" (p. 77). She was crying because she realized the Baby Jesus was poor, and from a "no account" family, and pushed into a corner, and overlooked, and despised and rejected, just like her.

And her brothers, Leroy, Claude, and Ollie, playing the three Wise Men, also went through a transformation. They proved it by giving the Baby Jesus the best thing they had.

Robinson writes again:

> *Everyone in the audience shifted around to watch the Wise Men march up the aisle.*
>
> *"What have they got?" Alice whispered.*
>
> *I didn't know, but whatever it was, it was heavy — Leroy almost dropped it. He didn't have his frankincense jar either, and Claude and Ollie didn't have anything although they were supposed to bring the gold and the myrrh.*
>
> *"I knew this would happen," Alice said for the second time. "I bet it's something awful."*
>
> *"Like what?"*
>
> *"Like ... a burnt offering. You know the Herdmans."*
>
> *Well, they did burn things. But they hadn't burnt this yet. It was a ham — and right away I knew where it came from. My father was on the church charitable works committee — they gave away food baskets at Christmas, and this was the Herdmans' food-basket ham ...*
>
> *"I'll bet they stole that!" Alice said.*
>
> *"They did not. It came from their food basket ..."*
>
> *[The Herdmans] had never before in their lives given anything away except lumps on the head. So you had to be impressed.*[1] — pp. 75-76

God coming down, down, down, and becoming a Baby had touched even the hardened hearts of the Herdmans. The wonder of Christmas is the wonder of God willingly choosing to put on human flesh, to "get into the tank," to become one of us, even to take *our* sins upon himself: to be born and live and suffer and die — and be raised again — so that we might live.

The Best Christmas "Pageant" *ever* will *always* be the first one. Nothing we can do can ever equal the pageantry, and majesty, and splendor of God's self-emptying, self-sacrificing love. No big extravaganza — moving and valuable though they are — can ever completely capture that wonder.

The best you and I can do is to receive it with thanksgiving and joy: with Imogene Herdman's tears of gratitude and with Leroy, Claude, and Ollie Herdman's gift of the very best that they had. And with skinny-legged, dirty-sneakered Gladys Herdman's shout of wonder: "Hey! Unto you a child is born!" (p. 80).

----

1. Copyright © 1972 by Barbara Robinson. Used by permission of HarperCollins Publishers.

A Christmas That Lasts

Luke 2:1-20

I would imagine that any one of us here this morning could tell an amusing story or two about unusual items that we have received at Christmas. At one time or another, most adults have gotten gifts that they consider just a little bit odd: like a battery-operated tie that flashes in the dark, or a water-proofed radio to play in the shower, or a year's supply of Norwegian sardines.

My family once received something unusual in a Christmas card. I opened up the envelope and along with the card, this packet fell out. On one side it reads: "Sprouts Birth of Jesus. Drop capsule in warm water and watch!" On the other side it continues, "Fun, educational, non-toxic, for children five years old and older. Not be taken internally. Each capsule contains a different figure: Mary-Joseph-Baby Jesus-Crèche ... Cross Publishing Company. Made in the USA."

What we have here is a clear plastic wrapper containing four pill-sized capsules. When you place the capsules in warm water, the capsule dissolves. And four sponge figurines, which have been packed tightly into the capsules, break out. Here's Mary, Joseph, the crèche, and the Baby Jesus. Christmas in a capsule. What will they think of next?

The little toy provides a moment of amusement and diversion. But when you come right down to it, it's kind of lightweight, disposable, easily lost, discarded, or forgotten. It treats the Nativity as a novelty and little more.

Sadly, some folks will experience a Christmas that has little more substance or permanence than one of these sponge-rubber figures. A Christmas equally capsulized. A Christmas not taken internally. A Christmas that is a mere novelty and little more.

In just a few days, once the scraps of wrapping paper are finally picked up off the living room floor, and the leftovers are eaten, and the guests have gone home, and the tree is taken down, then, for some folks, Christmas will be over until next December. Nothing will be left of Christmas — except the unpaid bills!

I think that's a shame! On the other hand, I believe it is possible to have a lasting Christmas, a Christmas that means as much to us in July as it means right now. One component of a Christmas that lasts is a continuing sense of wonder: the miracle of Almighty God emptying God's self, taking the form of a Servant, coming down to earth as a helpless infant, born in the likeness of human beings; the sudden appearance of the angelic chorus to the astonished shepherds out in the fields, the marvelous journey of the Wise Men to lay their treasures at the feet of an unknown peasant child in a dirty cattle stall. When we think about the elements of the Nativity story, we find, with Mary, that there is much to "ponder in our hearts." Christmas ought to give us "a rebirth of wonder."

But that sense of wonder and surprise need not be confined to Christmas. For the mysteries of God are there to be savored all of the year. I once read about an entomologist, a scientist who studies insects, who had spent his entire career studying a certain type of beetle. Turns out he was one of the world's foremost authorities on this particular beetle.

For decades, this scientist had devoted his life to the study of this insect, capturing it in the woods, breeding it in the laboratory, putting them under a microscope, publishing papers about them. Frankly, I initially thought it was kind of a weird way to spend your life. Any past or present entomologists here this morning, please don't take offense.

But after I thought a while, I realized that this man had a really healthy perspective. He was a Christian. And it was his belief that in finding out as much as he could about this particular beetle, he was helping to bring glory to God. God, after all, was the One who had fashioned these insects. The scientist wrote another thing I found interesting. He wrote that even after a lifetime of study, he felt he had barely scratched the surface in understanding his subject. He was still amazed as to how complex this insect was. It remained a marvel and a mystery to him.

Another scientist, Albert Einstein, once wrote: "The most beautiful thing we can experience is the mysterious. It is the source of all true art and science. He to whom this emotion is a stranger, who can no longer pause to wonder and stand wrapped in awe is as good as dead; his eyes are closed."

The Creator's wonders are all around us, from the tiniest insect to the vast reaches of the heavens and ocean, to a fragile flake of snow. All we need to do is open our eyes! The mysteries of Christ's birth remind us that life is bigger than our precise calculations and neat explanations. A continuing sense of wonder is a component of a Christmas that lasts.

So also is a lively belief in the existence of things spiritual. Christmas also is about the breaking into our world of a largely unseen world, the world of the spirit. It reminds us that there are truths beyond the truths we take for granted. As we ponder the Nativity story, it ought to have the effect of enlarging the horizons of our minds.

Take the existence of angels, for example. During Christmas, we hear about angels, we sing about angels, we hang angels on our trees. But then we tend to put them aside for another year. But the scriptures speak, nearly one hundred times, about the existence of angels. They are portrayed as God's messengers and our personal helpers. The Nativity reminds us of spiritual possibilities beyond our everyday world. Now, I don't know whether you believe in angels or not. Many Americans do ... about seventy percent.

Angels are a "hot" topic right now. Could you at least consider the possibility that angels exist? There's a lot of anecdotal evidence that they do.

I think about a story I read in *Time* magazine. It's the story of an angelic encounter, told by a woman named Ann Cannady.

Cannady is the second wife of a retired Air Force Master Sergeant named Gary who had lost his first wife to cancer. It turned out, after some years of marriage, that Ann Cannady was diagnosed as having advanced cancer herself. Of course, both she and her husband were crushed. They spent the weeks before a pending operation for her scared and praying. Ann prayed, "Please [God], if I'm going to die, let me die quickly. I don't want Gary to have to face this again."

Ann is convinced her prayers were answered. One morning, three days before she was to enter the hospital for surgery, Gary answered the door. Standing on the step was a large man, a good inch taller than her 6-foot, five-inch husband. "He was the blackest black I've ever seen," says Ann, "and his eyes were a deep, deep azure blue." The stranger introduced himself simply as Thomas. Then he told her that her cancer was gone.

Ann, still confused, looked at the man and demanded, "Who are you?"

He responded, "I am Thomas. I am sent by God."

Next, Ann recalls, "He held up his right hand, palm facing me, and leaned toward me, though he didn't touch me." The heat coming out of his hand, she reports, was incredible. Suddenly she felt her legs go out from under her and she fell to the floor. As she lay there, a strong white light, like a searchlight, traveled through her body. When she awoke, Thomas was gone and her husband was standing over her, asking her if she were still alive and begging her to speak.

Ann was convinced that Thomas was an angel visitor and that she had been healed. Her doctor was skeptical and put it down as stress. Still, at her insistence, he conducted a biopsy before subjecting her to the operation. The doctor discovered, much to his amazement, that the cancer was completely gone. It has not returned for fifteen years!

There are lots of stories about the existence of angels. To me, Ann's story, and others like it, reinforce the idea that the biblical account of angelic visitors is literally true. That's *my* opinion. You might share it, or not. But Christmas reminds us that there *are* truths beyond the truth that we take for granted. Who knows when one of God's angels might appear — maybe even to you!

Too often we experience a disposable, throw-away Christmas. A Christmas with about as much substance as one of these toys. But I contend that Christmas is not meant to be packed away, capsulized into one month, or maybe five weeks, and then *forgotten*. Christmas is meant to give us a new perspective on life. When we look at the things of this world with a renewed sense of wonder, when we have a lively belief in things spiritual, we bring something of Christmas into our daily living. We break Christmas out of its capsule and begin to experience a *Christmas* that *lasts*.

The Christ Child And The Angels: A Story Sermon

Luke 2:22-24, 39-40

This particular Sunday is one of those Sundays that presents a preacher with what I call "an embarrassment of riches." There is *so much* that one could preach about this week. It's kind of hard to select a single theme! We're still in Christmastide. The sound of Christmas carols is ringing in our ears. Some of the Christmas decorations are still up in the sanctuary. So, do you preach about Christmas? Or, since it's January 1, the first Sunday, the first day of a new year, do you preach on something related to New Year's, say like resolutions for the New Year? It's also a Communion Sunday. The table of bread and wine speak to us of impending death by crucifixion. It's also a Food Collection Sunday, a Sunday that reminds us of the needs of others. Do you preach about the believer's responsibility to reach out to the poor in the New Year in the name of our Savior, Christ?

To some extent, our religious symbols seem to be at odds this Sunday, focusing on different aspects of the life of Jesus. Christmastide, the joyful celebration of Jesus' birth, and the Lord's Supper, the solemn remembrance of his death, might seem to clash. But there is one element that holds a lot of these themes together. In both his birth and death, Jesus *sacrificed* himself. Jesus gave something up for us. And he did so out of love.

That's quite clear in the crucifixion. But, God coming down to earth, living among us, suffering all our common, daily irritations and disappointments and pains — that, too, is a form of self-sacrifice. The Incarnation, as well as the Crucifixion, speaks plainly of God's love. The love of Christ for us, Jesus' giving himself for us, is the subject of both our Christmas decorations and our celebration of the Lord's Supper. It's also the subject of the little story I'd like to tell. It's called, "The Christ Child and the Angels." It goes like this ...

Jesus and Mary and Joseph were well cared for in the eight days they passed in the stable behind the inn in Bethlehem. The shepherds brought cheese, bread, fruit, and firewood. Their wives and daughters cared for Jesus until Mary was back on her feet. But at the end of that week, after they had visited the Temple in Jerusalem nearby for the dedication of their firstborn child, it was time for the little family to return to their home in the village of Nazareth. Mary and Joseph packed their meager belongings, bundled up the baby Jesus, and set forth with their donkey for the long and dusty trip.

It was hot on the journey. Mary held the baby Jesus in her arms while Joseph led the donkey. About noontime on the first day, they stopped to rest in a little wood. And immediately, from behind the trees, appeared a band of tiny angels. They were chubby youngsters with pink, round faces. They looked for all the world like Cabbage Patch Kids with wings.

Yet in spite of their young age, they were alert and vigorous and could do quite a lot — much more than the average child could be expected to do. Oh, and one more thing: they were invisible, except to Mary and Joseph, and to the Baby Jesus, of course.

The little angels began to serve the Holy Family. They brought Mary and Joseph jars of fresh water and ripe fruits that they had gathered by flying to nearby orchards. They offered Mary a bouquet of fresh-picked flowers and provided a comfortable pile of tree boughs for her to sit on. And when the Holy Family resumed their journey, the little band of angels flew along. Several carried Joseph's burdens. Others took turns leading the donkey. In general they looked after all of Mary and Joseph and the baby Jesus' needs.

After the family returned to its humble, white-washed home on a side street in Nazareth, the little angels continued to fuss over Mary and Joseph and the baby. When Mary awoke in the morning, she found that the angels had already started breakfast, swept out the kitchen, and dusted the entire house. When Joseph went into his carpenter's shop to work, the angels picked up the wood shavings and chips, tidied up around his work bench, and handed him his tools. Joseph never had to worry about hitting his thumb with a hammer because the little angels held the nails!

Plus, the angels tended to all the needs of the baby Jesus. When Jesus was wet, they changed him immediately. When it was his nap time, they flew him gently to his cradle and rocked him to sleep. There was nothing that the little band of angels wouldn't do for the Holy Family. They adored Jesus and were just happy to have the privilege of serving the Son of God.

Now, you would have thought this arrangement was great for Mary and Joseph and the baby. At least Joseph had to admit that he liked it pretty well. Joseph was quite a bit older than Mary, you might remember, and even though he was kind and good-hearted, in his advancing years he was getting a little bit tired of working. Joseph really appreciated the extra help the angels gave.

But Mary, sensitive Mary, introspective Mary, who kept all things and pondered them in her heart, was disquieted. After several weeks had gone by, Mary began to feel that something was wrong. And with that sixth sense that mothers have, Mary knew that the baby Jesus felt it, too. He was appreciative, but sort of restless when the angels were tending him, almost as if he were struggling with something in his infant mind.

Mary began to sense that the little angels, loving and gentle as they were, adoring as they were, might be doing Jesus a disservice. And so Mary decided to insist that the little angels stop doing their helpful tasks.

One morning, as she was getting up, she saw the angels sweeping out her bedroom. Mary quietly took the broom away. Later that morning, she observed two of the angels rocking Jesus' cradle during his morning nap. She asked them to stop and rocked him herself. Then Mary refused to let the angels carry her wash to the washhouse. And when Joseph came in for lunch, she suggested that he turn the angels out of his shop.

"Whatever for?" Joseph wanted to know. (You see, Joseph had come to enjoy them.)

"Because Jesus is the Messiah, the Chosen One, the Son of the Living God," Mary responded.

"But," said Joseph, "isn't it only natural that God's Son should be served by angels?"

"No!" Mary insisted. "Don't you know that the Messiah has come to earth, not be served, but to serve and to share our common lot? The Messiah is here to suffer with men and women, to experience all the hardship and losses and challenges that all of us must face. And that includes the discomforts of babies. You and I must begin tending and providing for Jesus by ourselves."

Joseph saw her wisdom and, with a touch of sadness, agreed.

Of course, this new arrangement was a tremendous disappointment for the little angels. Late that afternoon, Mary saw them gathered in the courtyard at the back of the house, huddled under a fig tree, their little shoulders shaking as they sobbed huge tears. Their little hearts seemed to be broken.

So Mary tried to explain to them that this really was the wish of the baby Jesus. She told the angels she could understand their disappointment. But she also suggested that they could do something that would please Jesus very much.

"Down the street," she said, "you'll find old Elizabeth. She's paralyzed on one side. Help her with her washing. And then there's Rachael, with her twelve children. One of them always needs to be rocked or changed or watched. There's Stephen, who is blind. Help him by cleaning up around his house. And poor Anna, almost too poor to pay the rent. Bring her some food." Soon Mary had scattered the angels around Nazareth, where they became equally busy tending the needs of the sick and the poor.

All that year, the needy of Nazareth were tended by the invisible angelic servants. In fact, the people of Nazareth still speak of that year as "The Year When Not One Baby Cried." Not a single baby cried!

Except, of course, for the baby named Jesus who lived in the house of the carpenter, Joseph, with his young wife, Mary. He alone cried, for Jesus had chosen to suffer for them all.

Story adapted from "The Virgin and the Angels" by Jules LeMataire, [1853-1914] as found in *Stories of Christ and Christmas,* Edward Wagenkencht, editor, David McKay Company, Inc.

Wise Men — And Women —
Still Seek Him

Matthew 2:1-11

My sister once sent these verses as part of her annual Christmas letter:

"'Tis the week after Christmas and all through the house, not a package was still wrapped, not even a blouse. The stockings are picked up from the chimney where they fell; the children are fighting and starting to yell. Yes fighting and yelling and calling their dreads; the sugar they've eaten has gone to their heads! The excitement of New Year's has finally passed. And the Bowl games are over. Back to normal at last!"

It does seem as if the holidays are over, doesn't it? But, technically speaking, we're still in Christmastide. In the church year, the season of Christmas is twelve days long. Remember the old song, "The Twelve Days Of Christmas"? Christmas doesn't officially end until Epiphany, January 6. So it's still appropriate to sing some Christmas carols and to hear a sermon about Christmas. On this the Second Sunday after Christmas, we generally think about the Wise Men and their contribution to the Christmas story.

We're all familiar with the story of the Three Kings, having seen dozens of Christmas pageants with ten-year-old boys dressed up as kings, wearing royal crowns made out of cardboard and royal robes made out of their fathers' bathrobes.

Actually scripture doesn't say anywhere that they were kings, does it? More likely they were court astrologers from ancient Persia, which is modern-day Iraq. Scripture doesn't even say there were three of them, does it? We get the idea of three from the mention of three gifts.

But whoever they are, and however many they were, they were persons of importance. In the story when they arrive at Jerusalem, King Herod sees them right away. And there's another thing about them. They were honest seekers. Think about what they went through to get closer to God!

Inspired by the star in the sky, they left their homes and families and set off on a difficult and dangerous journey. They didn't know exactly where they were going. Can you imagine planning for such a journey? If you didn't know where you were going, how would you know what to pack? And how could you tell your family how long you'd be away?

Then there were the rigors of the journey itself. Through the burning sands and freezing nights of the Arabian Desert, rocking back and forth on their camels, through sandstorms and windstorms, under threat of robbers, they pushed on.

They finally arrived in Jerusalem, thinking their long journey was ended. They expected a big celebration, torches lit, trumpets blowing, people dancing in the streets, rejoicing in the birthday of a King. But not a soul was stirring. So, after a brief visit with Herod, they pushed on.

They pushed on to Bethlehem, following the star, seeking enlightenment. And what did they find there at the end of their trip? No royal robes or royal entourage or palace, but just a peasant baby, born of poor parents, cradled in a manger in a smelly shack. The whole experience of seeking and encountering the Christ Child must have been confusing for the Wise Men. But notice how they kept at it. In faith, they completed their mission, laying out their expensive treasures at the poor baby's feet.

The Wise Men represent men and women from every age who are seekers: sincere folks who long to know God, who will sacrifice to try to understand God, who are serious about growing in devotion and faith. The Wise Men were seekers. And I'm sure that at one level or another, all of us here this morning are seekers too. Isn't that what has brought us to worship: a desire to know more about God, a hope to draw closer to God?

And aren't we fortunate! We don't have to travel across a desert, following a star, risking our lives, to make contact with Jesus. We can find fellowship with Jesus, we can worship Jesus, and we can receive Jesus into ourselves by sharing this morning in the Supper of our Lord. For the Child of Bethlehem, the Man of Jerusalem, the DayStar, the Risen Jesus is here with us in the bread and the cup. Led on by the star, the Wise Men sought Jesus; the Wise Men went to Jesus. Now Jesus comes to us in communion. Wise men and women seek him here.

Here we see God, God's sacrifice for our sins represented in a broken body; God's love and forgiveness for us poured out in Christ's blood. Here we are invited to take God's strength and goodness into ourselves. Here our differences and divisions are overcome and healed. Here we can forgive each other, make up with each other, and are reunited with each other. Here, in some special way, we draw close to God.

Wise men and women seek Jesus in communion. In this sacrament we are offered what sent the Wise Men on their journey, the kind of closeness to God, the understanding of God, the vision of God that men and women, down through the ages, have longed for and sought.

What are you searching for? Could it be the same thing the Wise Men were searching for: closeness to God? I believe we can find both strength for our journey and the fulfillment of our journey in a relationship with Jesus, through the Sacrament of Communion — here.

Be Born In Us Today

Luke 2:1-20

A family was gathered together around their Advent wreath in preparation for Christmas. "Who can tell me what the four candles on the Advent wreath mean?" Mother asked. Her seven-year-old son jumped right in, "They stand for Love, Joy, Peace, and ... and ... and ... "

His older sister finished his sentence; "They stand for Love, Joy, and Peace and Quiet!"

Although the little girl was technically wrong — the missing candle stands for Hope — she still had a point. In many of our homes, Peace and Quiet can be missing around Christmas. The days of December, meant to be merry, can be the most harried days of our year.

One of those "magazine shows," *Dateline NBC*, once ran a segment titled "The Nightmare before Christmas" (12/20/95). A camera crew followed a family of six from suburban New Jersey as they waded their way through Advent. Two exhausted, over-worked parents (especially Mom, who was doing most of the work); four over-stimulated, demanding kids, shoving and screaming in the mini-van; $2,000 spent on Christmas gifts in overcrowded stores, all were caught on camera. It wasn't a pretty picture. But it was an accurate reminder of what the Christmas season can be like.

I thought it might be interesting to separate the celebration of Christ's birth from December 25. *Why not* Christmas in July? In point of fact, we don't know the exact birthdate of Jesus. Does that shock you? Pope Julius officially established December 25 as Christmas in 350 A.D.

Under the old Roman calendar (slightly different from ours) December 25 was the winter solstice, the shortest, darkest day of

113

the year. A lot of pagan partying, including excessive eating and drinking, took place on and around December 25 (does that sound familiar?). So the Pope proclaimed the winter solstice the Birthday of Jesus. It was a powerful reminder that Christ is the Light of the World, a Light that shines in the darkness, which the darkness cannot overcome. But the date was made up.

We are free to celebrate the birth of Jesus any day we want, including in July. Some merchants have already caught on to this, by the way. If you rush out to any Hallmark Greeting Card store this afternoon you will catch the tail end of the "unveiling" of Hallmark's Christmas Ornament Collection! We can do our Christmas ornament shopping five months early! Merry Christmas from Hallmark Greeting Cards (who, like God, "cares enough to send the very best!").

As I thought about this service, a verse from "O Little Town of Bethlehem" kept running through my head:

> *O holy Child of Bethlehem! descend to us, we pray;*
> *Cast out our sin and enter in; be born in us today.*
> *We hear the Christmas angels the great glad tidings*
>   *tell;*
> *O come to us, abide with us, our Lord Emmanuel!"*

Wouldn't it be wonderful if Jesus could be born in us, in some new way, each and every day? He *was* born of the Virgin Mary once. But Jesus can also be born in us, again and again. It depends on whether you or I have what Stuart Brisco calls "The Spirit of Christmas" *or* "The Spirit of Christ" ("Christmas 365 Days a Year," *Preaching Today,* tape no. 135). What's the difference between these two?

The "Spirit of Christmas" is that warm, fuzzy feeling of "peace on earth and good will to women and men" that we usually get around the holidays. We give the Salvation Army bell ringer not just our leftover change but a whole dollar! We give generously to other charities, too. We smile at strangers, hum Christmas carols, and are generally uplifted. We don't even get angry when someone pushes in front of us in line at the Christmas Tree Shop! (Sometimes.)

The "Spirit of Christmas" is powerful. But it passes. "The Spirit of Christ," on the other hand, "Emmanuel," "God with us" *can be* a daily event. What *can* happen to you and me is similar to what happened to Mary. The Holy Spirit came upon Mary. Christ was born in her.

Of course, Mary's experience of the indwelling Christ was unique! *She* had morning sickness! But, also the thrill when the Child first moved within her. Plus the feeling that many pregnant women report that while they're pregnant, they're never alone. Everything they eat and everything they do is done with and for somebody else.

What Mary felt, the biological bonding with the Christ Child, you and I can never feel. Still, "The Spirit of Christ," the Holy Spirit, *can* be born in us today, and every day. Some experience the Holy Spirit as overpowering, like the "slain in the Spirit" Pentecostals in Robert Duvall's movie, *The Apostle*. Others, like Robert Duvall himself, experience the Spirit as "a certain quiet, emotional uplift ... a stillness, more than any kind of noisy exaltation ... a 'still, small voice,' " (*Newsweek*, April 13, 1998, p. 60). But whether the Spirit comes to us as Wind and Fire or as a "still, small voice," Jesus promised us the Holy Spirit as our Helper (John 14:16). If we don't experience the Spirit, might it be because we haven't invited the Spirit in?

Mary said, "Behold, I am the handmaid of the Lord; let it be to me according to your word" (Luke 1:38 RSV). She turned her life — and her body — over to God. I wonder what wonders might begin to happen in your and my life if you and I got up each morning and said, *really meaning it*, "Behold, I am the servant of the Lord. Let it be to me today according to your word."

But do we make time to invite "The Spirit of Christ" into our day? Noted author Madeleine L'Engle does. She writes in *A Circle Of Quiet* (Seabury Press) about her "special place ... a small brook in a green glade ... from which there is no visible sign of human beings. There's a natural stone bridge over the brook," and she sits there, "dangling [her] legs and looking through the foliage at the sky reflected in the water, and things slowly come back into perspective." She continues, "If the insects are biting me — and they usually are; no place is quite perfect — I use the pliable branch of a shad-blow tree as a fan."

She continues, "The brook wanders through a tunnel of foliage, and the birds sing more sweetly there than anywhere else ... and I move slowly into a kind of peace that is marvelous, annihilating all that's made to a green thought in a green shade" (p. 4). Young Mary took all things and "pondered them in her heart" (Luke 2:19). The Baby Jesus was born in her. Middle-age (when she wrote that) Madeleine L'Engle escaped to a green glade. Helpful, spiritual books were born in her. Have *we* established a place of daily "peace and quiet" where we can meet the "Spirit of Christ?" Who knows what the Spirit might do in us and through us, if we gave it half a chance.

What that means is putting up in our lives one of those signs you sometimes see in stores: UNDER NEW MANAGEMENT. We're *under new management* if we invite the Spirit of Christ into our lives. Our circumstances may not change. The shepherds went back to tending their sheep — good thing for the sheep! In the eleventh century, King Henry III of Bavaria tired of being king and applied to become a contemplative at a local monastery. The prior met the king at the door and asked, "Your Majesty, do you understand that the pledge here is one of obedience? That will be hard because you have been king."

"I understand," said King Henry, "for the rest of my life, I will be obedient ... as Christ leads you."

"Then," said the prior, "go back to your throne and serve faithfully in the place where God has put you." When he died, it was written of King Henry, "[He] learned to rule by being obedient."

King Henry's circumstances did not change. But his attitude did. From then on, he was *under new management*. His life belonged to Christ. And we don't have to be people of power to be useful. God made excellent use of an obedient peasant girl named Mary, and of a faithful carpenter named Joseph.

The late Mother Teresa wrote, "It is Christmas every time you smile at your brother (or sister) and offer [them] your hand. It is

Christmas every time you remain silent and listen to another. It is Christmas every time you turn your back on the principles that oppress the poor. It is Christmas every time you hope with the 'prisoners.' It is Christmas every time you recognize in humility your limitations. It is Christmas every time you let God love others through you." (*Life in the Spirit*, Harper and Row, p. 73.)

Howard Thurman, a great African-American preacher from another generation, puts it another way:

> *When the song of the angel is stilled,*
> *When the star in the sky is gone,*
> *When the kings and princes are home,*
> *When the shepherds are back with their flocks;*
> *The work of Christmas begins;*
> *To find the lost,*
> *To heal the broken,*
> *To feed the hungry,*
> *To release the prisoner,*
> *To rebuild the nations,*
> *To bring peace among people,*
> *To make music with the heart ...*
>
> *O holy Child of Bethlehem! descend to us, we pray;*
> *Cast out our sin and enter in: be born in us today.*
> *We hear the Christmas angels the great glad tidings tell;*
> *O come to us, abide with us, our Lord Emmanuel!*

Christmas is not just about December 25, and parties and presents. Christmas is about a Living Presence, "The Spirit Of Christ," "Emmanuel," "God with us," every day. Today you and I can make a place for the Christ Child. He doesn't have to stay "Away In A Manger" in a "Little Town Of Bethlehem." He can be born in us, and live in us, and work God's will through us, every day. *If we* establish a place of peace and quiet, if we put ourselves *under new management*, if we say daily "Behold, we are the servants of the Lord. Let it be to us according to your word."